Divorce Mediation

THE RATIONAL ALTERNATIVE

Dr. Howard H. Irving

PERSONAL LIBRARY PUBLISHERS

Toronto

D0123354

Personal Library, Publishers
Suite 439
17 Queen Street East
Toronto, Canada M5C 1P9

Publisher: Glenn Edward Witmer
Editor: Dorothy Martins
Production Editor: Catherine Van Baren
Design: First Image
Composition: Video Text Inc.

Distributed to the trade by
John Wiley and Sons Canada Limited
22 Worcester Road
Rexdale, Ontario M9W 1L1

Canadian Cataloguing in Publication Data

Irving, Howard H.

Divorce Mediation
Bibliography: p. 208
Includes Index.

ISBN 0-920510-03-5

1. Divorce.   I. Title.

HQ814.I79   306.8'9   C80-094105-5

Printed and bound in Canada

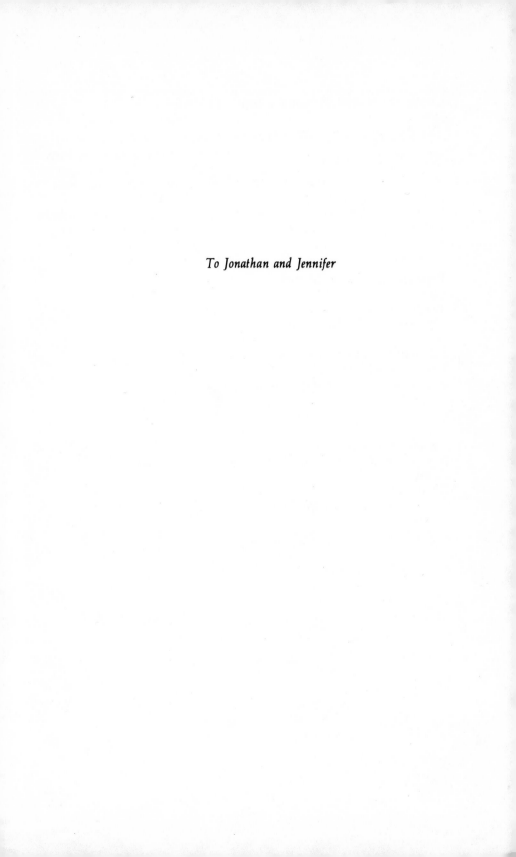

To Jonathan and Jennifer

Table of Contents

ACKNOWLEDGMENTS

This must begin with my invaluable contacts at the Los Angeles Conciliation Court where Meyer Elkin, the past director, gave me the inspiration for writing this book. I am deeply indebted to him. James MacDonald, a family lawyer, showed me the value of divorce mediation from a legal perspective. This was especially helpful, both in my own personal situation and in a professional way. To the many clients who shared with me their pain and courage, I am truly grateful.

My professional colleagues who worked with me and contributed directly or indirectly to the book were many; Ben Schlesinger, Peter Bohm, Ernie Lightman, Michael Benjamin and Ralph Garber, to mention a few. I thank them for their expert knowledge.

Jim Wills and Dorothy Martins gave me the editorial assistance which made this book far more readable. I am deeply appreciative.

The numerous and lengthy discussions with Leslie Michener helped me gain a better perspective. For her support, I am truly indebted.

My publisher, Glenn Witmer, had the patience and knowledge to help make this book a reality. I hope I have done him justice.

Finally, to my children, Jonathan and Jennifer, who above all taught me the real value of divorce mediation, I only hope that I was a good student.

PREFACE

There is a growing disenchantment among judges, lawyers, litigants, and behavioral scientists with the current adversarial method of resolving family disputes. Although the mechanical separation and legal technicalities are taken care of, little is done about the emotional trauma that the husband, wife, and their children are going through.

The filing for a divorce often intensifies family conflict, and the adversarial approach tends to polarize the parties as it automatically places litigants at opposite ends of the domestic ring—and almost forces them "to put on boxing gloves." It makes them unnecessary combatants, prolongs the conflicts, interferes with future relationships between the parties, and even worse, between the parents and their children. When one party starts to fight, the other party will likely respond automatically and fight back: action and reaction. The growing list of those who find fault with the adversary system agree that it is too impersonal, causes undue stress and anxiety, doesn't respect privacy, is unresponsive to the emotional problems involved, and is costly and time consuming. Although "legal rights" may be protected, "emotional rights" are ignored.

Unfortunately, matrimonial cases do not always end with the divorce decree. Some spouses continue to pursue each other through the court system, fighting over visitation, custody, child support payments, alimony, and other harassing litigation. With parents who part as enemies, child visitation and custody may be the battle-ground for continuing their fight after the dissolution is granted. No wonder there is a growing search for

11

a better and more humane way of separating people who no longer love each other.

The courts have begun to take note of the emotional trauma involved in the separation process and the relatively recent Conciliation Court movement is an attempt to bring a "humanization" to divorces. Conciliation Courts are a marriage of the behavioral sciences and the law. In this service run by the courts, counselors try to preserve the marriage by emphasizing strengths and assets that may still exist. If the marriage cannot be saved, the counselor tries to terminate it in a way that is least detrimental to the parents and their children. Although established with a focus on avoiding unnecessary dissolutions, Conciliation Court counseling also helps the parties to accept the divorce, to emotionally prepare for its consequences and change of lifestyle and to part with a sense of dignity and self-worth, with less trauma to themselves and their children. However, it does not normally get into the resolution of property or other rights.

Dr. Howard Irving offers divorce mediation as an alternative method of settling family disputes without litigation. It's an alternative option to the adversary system and is a *self-determining* process for resolving issues resulting from divorce. Mediation provides a framework for divorcing couples *themselves* to determine and agree on their respective responsibilities after the divorce. If the parties are able to agree on division of their property, custody, child support, and similar matters, this will decrease the chances of future litigation and they can then go about the important job of rebuilding their lives.

Dr. Irving presents both a plea and a plan for a more rational, constructive and humane approach to conflicts that may occur during the divorce. He provides a thoughtful critique of the abuses inherent in the adversarial approach to divorce and family dissolution and argues that the adversary system should be the *last resort* rather than the first. He makes a persuasive argument that the adversarial approach often fails to serve the best interest of the divorcing couple and their children and perpetuates disequilibrium by projecting blame, encouraging retaliation, generating resentment, increasing tensions and creating a win-lose confrontation.

This book offers an alternative, in divorce mediation, which focuses on the current relationships and provides a mutual framework for negotiation, compromise and resolution of differences for the good of *all* family members. The author, who has a fine background as a writer, lecturer, professor, and extensive "on-the-line" training in family counseling, makes a forceful case that mediation has many advantages and is a vast improvement over the practice that makes adversaries out of divorcing husbands and wives. He recognizes the role of the legal profession in mediation and in helping to establish a more rational approach to divorce as well as the need for more family law specialists and lawyers who are equipped to work with and refer divorcing couples for conciliation counseling and mediation.

Any alternative that helps to take the emotional strain and bitterness out of the divorce process and which will avoid lengthy court battles is an approach that deserves thoughtful consideration. The admirable goal of divorce mediation is to provide a basis whereby marriages can be terminated without destroying the couple or their children and reflects ancient religious law in which the intent was not only to dispense justice but to make peace among the litigants.

This book presents a forthright analysis of a difficult and troublesome subject, and Dr. Irving has made a needed contribution.

Judge Norman S. Fenton
Presiding Judge of the Conciliation Court
Superior Court
Tucson, Arizona

Chapter One

THE ODDS ARE

A major goal of divorce mediation is to help the couple become rational and responsible enough to co-operate towards making compromises which are acceptable to both people. Voluntary settlements, worked out by the spouses on both an emotional level as well as an intellectual one, are not only more humane than those forced by litigation, but they are also more practical. Mutual agreement means that neither party is the "loser" and that neither has been taken advantage of. Eliminating blame also lessens the possibility of the revenge factor erupting later and leading to prolonged legal battles.

The oddsmakers will give you odds on almost everything: who will win the next election, what football team will make the Rose Bowl, whether or not a certain stock will rise or fall. Odds are calculated on statistical probability and, if you are married, the probability of your being one of the two principal parties in a divorce action are *one in four.* If you are simply living and breathing in North America the odds of your being involved with someone who is getting a divorce are better than *even.*

Just about everyone has had, or will have, the experience of standing by while relatives or close friends go through the painful process of divorce. Perhaps you have just met an old friend on the street and invite him or her to dinner. Casually, you include the marital partner in the invitation. There is an awkward silence, followed by the confession that they are separated, getting a divorce, or no longer in contact. In all probability this will lead to your hearing one side of the story. You are duly confused because *both* of these people are your friends. You stumble for the right words and inwardly you choose whether or not to become involved. This is the casual experience with divorce–many people will experience it more intimately.

This book is about divorce mediation. It is not a "how to" book, but rather a "how you might proceed" book. It is written for the principal parties in marriage breakdown, for their relatives and friends, for their children, and for professionals working in the field, in a style that will articulate its message for multiple audiences.

This year alone in North America over one million marriages will end. Three quarters of these will involve children. All will affect "satellite" figures: grandparents, brothers and sisters, friends. Divorce directly influences a whole system of people in addition to the principal parties. Conservatively, five million people will be closely tied to these one million divorces. The nuclear family (mother, father and children) appears to be more extended than we usually acknowledge. People who sometimes seem uninvolved when all is well become quite involved when things go wrong.

Although it is fashionable to discuss "the death of the family," the family remains the basic unit of our society. The family is still the primary source of psychological security and personality development. The function of the family is obvious to the specialists, or agents of society who pick up the pieces after family breakdown. Judges, lawyers, the police, social workers, psychiatrists and others deal daily with the psychological and sociological consequences of family breakdown. The consequences include personal alienation, increased child abuse, kidnapping, juvenile delinquency, and second generation divorce to mention only a few.[1]

Divorce litigation is unique among legal actions because it is invariably accompanied by intense and intimate emotions. Divorce is rarely a clean piece of business with a clear-cut beginning and end. Seldom can it be handled and simply filed away. Divorce is a painful process for all concerned. When psychological factors which affect the situation are not dealt with throughout the divorce process, the resulting complications come back to plague the parties. There may be bitter acrimony over child custody and visitation rights. There may be continued court actions over non-payment of alimony and child support.

The cost of divorce in human terms is incalculable. Dean Irving N. Griswold, of the Harvard Law School said, concerning domestic relations "There is some law here, of course, but the problems are essentially ones of human relations in their most intense and complex form."[2]

The final Divorce Decree document in one (U.S.) state proclaims that the parties are "fully restored to their former state." If only that were so! Occasionally, when there are no children involved, the couple simply parts company. Gradually, the wounds heal. More often than not, however, children *are* involved. The couple must go on seeing one another and the wounds caused by the divorce action are opened and reopened. What causes the wounds to be so deep? Why is a divorce one of the most serious of life's crises?

The answers to these two questions lie in our legal system as well as in the relationship of the couple. A divorce action, by tradition, finds fault. It rewards one of the parties and punishes the other. This is complicated by the fact that usually one of the parties desires the divorce more strongly than the other.

It seems paradoxical to have fault grounds and still hope to help the couple work constructively to mediate their differences. The retention of the fault grounds and the psychological impact of the adversary system results in pitting the marital couple against one another in mortal combat. It is a system that requires winners and losers. One of the parties is demeaned and made to feel guilty. This naturally causes retaliatory counterattacks. Given the emotional trauma which already exists in most cases, constructive communication between the spouses becomes even more difficult. In other words, people who are already at emotional risk and in need of support find themselves involved in a system which offers the opposite of what it might. They are caught in a downward emotional spiral.

How common is such a crisis? Here is a useful explanation of what may be referred to as "the seasons of stress."

"Just as common factors exist which evoke stress in the divorced, there are predictable stressful phases which divorced people experience as part of the continuing process of change. Stress affects the individual all along the road to divorce and after it: and the outcome of changing relationships, old and new, often depends on the individual's ability to deal with stress at the time and also to prepare for or avert the next phase of stress.

"Four definable periods are easily recognized: the stress of unresolved marital discord that leads to divorce; the stress of the divorce process itself; the stress of the immediate post-divorce period; and the stress of constructing a new life with new relationships. To generalize, it can be said that these stages comprise a continuum of potential stress, with stress at its lowest at the beginning of the process, rising to a crescendo during and immediately after the divorce, and then subsiding again as a new life eventually emerges. The time involved varies considerably. It is especially difficult to know how long a divorce is in the making, although it is accepted that it takes an individual, on the average, at least two years to form new and lasting relationships within or without a new marriage. Thus the whole process is long and the individual endures sustained stress.

"The making of a divorce is almost always stressful. The slow, painful, deterioration of the relationship causes suffering as two individuals try again and again to patch up and start over and to keep control over their destiny. With each failure, they experience the slipping away of a life on which they have based all their hopes and into which they have poured all their energies. Many troubled marriages can be, and are saved. They are even stronger once the broken places are healed. So divorce is not inevitable in a problem marriage. But when sexual anxieties, disappointed expectations, destructive role-playing, and inability to grow or change–these are all common ingredients–are left unresolved, they give rise to sadness, anger, hate, frustration, and loneliness. The incompatibility and the disharmony become unbearable. Often what the mind cannot bear the body burdens, so that all the varieties of psychosomatic symptoms and illnesses cause further aggravation."[3]

Some marriages dissolve more quietly or more easily than others. But in the end, for many, divorce becomes the answer to a personal dilemma. As 90 percent of divorces are uncontested, it is frequently the best possible solution to the problem.

The effects of our legal system complicate and increase stress during three of the "four seasons of stress" described above. Justice Louis H. Burke, formerly of the Conciliation Court of Los Angeles said,

"... the adversary system as it applies to domestic relations falls short of the mark; it provides solely the knife to sever the nuptial knot. Furthermore, in every step, the adversary system has the effect of deepening marital wounds and rendering the possibility of reconciliation increasingly more difficult."[4]

Let's begin with the divorce process itself. A major cause of pain in most divorces is the fact that both parties are seldom at the same level of readiness to terminate the marriage. One inevitably consults a lawyer first. Most commonly, one of the partners has left or is about to leave. The other party feels rejected and abandoned. The rejected spouse who is unable to accept the fact that his or her partner will really go through with the divorce is frequently willing to agree to almost anything in the vain hope that this will bring the spouse back. It is not uncommon for a spouse in this situation to try to have the marriage counselor make an effort to get the estranged spouse to come back. The following case illustrates the conflicting emotions of one client.

Mrs. Brown was desperate. She began by trying to impress me with what a wonderful person her estranged spouse was. At the same time, she was giving me factual information as to how he plotted and planned his leaving. He had transferred all his assets into a corporation name. He also had several meetings with his lawyers and purchased a home in the name of his new girlfriend. Mrs. Brown's trauma was intensified because she had found this out from her son, rather than from her spouse.

With all of these facts and because she was emotionally distraught, Mrs. Brown was unable to function rationally. She felt prepared to accept little or no maintenance in order not to jeopardize the chances for reconciliation. "I'm not concerned about the money. I just want him back. You can't imagine how lonely I've been the past seven weeks," she cried.

The rejected party is often so upset by the realization that the spouse is actually leaving they cannot sort out what the real financial needs may be. Sometimes, depression is so great that an inadequate financial arrangement is accepted simply to get the whole procedure over and done with. Conversely, the guilt of the party who is leaving may be so great that an unreasonably high amount of maintenance is offered. Time passes and eventually resentment rises to the surface and results in further litigation.

The phrase, "I didn't want this divorce!" often implies, "I didn't cause this divorce," or, "I am not the one to blame." Revenge surfaces easily and proves the cliché that love and hate are two closely-related emotions. The adversary system serves revenge well. Legal punishment threatens the alleged guilty party. A case in point follows.

John Wilson was angry and resentful because his wife had left him. Worse yet, her new male companion had been a mutual friend. He was so infuriated that his main concern was to hurt his wife in the deepest way. He kept repeating over and over again that his wife was a tramp, an unfit mother, and that there was no way in which she would ever get their children.

It is typical for the spurned spouse to adopt the view that he or she has been made to suffer all sorts of indignities. The result is to seek revenge in the form of money, or much worse, by using the children as a means of punishing the spouse or "getting even."

Children are always the casualties of their parents' marital battles. They often become pawns in the struggle. Parents often use their children to salve their own bruised egos, or they vie for the children's favor. The children are thus forced into a conflict of loyalties and more often than not the struggle has permanent debilitating effects on their developing personalities.

The newly-separated parent in the midst of dealing with a sense of loss and isolation needs a great deal of support and energy to cope with children. Resentment is often forthcoming on the part of the non-custodial parent. At the same time, the parent with custody may use the children. By denying access, the custodial parent takes revenge on the guilty parent.

In one case, a child was unable to see his father on his scheduled weekend visit. When the father finally was able to visit with the child some weeks later, he encouraged the child not to return to his mother. When the 12-year-old boy visited my office, he pleaded with me to stop his parents hurting him. He described, in his words, the classic double bind: "If I agree with Mom, Dad gets mad at me, and when I agree with Dad, Mom gets mad. I think if they got back together, things would be a lot better."

Even when both parents are aware of these dangers and make a conscious effort to prevent them, their own high level of anxiety throughout the entire divorce process damages their parenting abilities. When the parents in the case above were confronted with what they were doing to their son, they were totally preoccupied with putting each other down and unable to appreciate how they were hurting the child. They wanted to cast him into the role of judge. Each blamed the other for the terrible situation. Each produced affidavits from their opposing lawyers in scathing denunciation of each other's ability to parent.

Typical accusations include "He comes home drunk most of the time and disrupts the children;" "She is totally irresponsible and allows the children to keep late hours and she never knows where they are most evenings."

The third "season of stress" is the post-divorce period. The pre-divorce period and the process of the divorce itself typically produce the kinds of emotional situations described above. The result is often post-divorce depression and is not unlike a mourning period. It can last for a considerable length of time. Is it simply a matter of sitting back and waiting for the emotional scars to heal? Is it all finally over? Unfortunately, the end of divorce proceedings often marks the beginning of legal problems. There may be seemingly endless litigation around child custody and visitation, non-payment of alimony and support.

The best known and most devastating court battle is the custody proceeding. The judge, with his wide discretionary powers, becomes the referee between the warring parties. Experience has shown that the effects of court custody decisions do not so much terminate the dispute as change them. Whereas before custody adjudication parents might battle over who will have the children, now they are likely to battle over the conditions of visitation.

One parent is given custody. The other is given visitation rights. If bitterness still exists between the parents, and it often does, the new arguments focus on visitation. The non-custodial parent may not be able to accept the judge's decision. He or she may create special problems by not picking up the children on time, or by bringing them back late. The custodial parent may then have a lawyer send off an affidavit to the effect that the non-custodial parent has violated the terms of the visiting rights. The parent with custody feels the other parent's behavior harms the children. He or she wants to prevent the other parent from seeing the children altogether. The cycle begins again. Old wounds are left open, the parents and children again return to court before still another judge and with yet another unresolved issue.

The continuing bitterness may result in one legal battle after another. The parties may become so paralyzed by their continuing battle that they are unable to begin building new lives. The children become property to be fought over and divided. Great emotional damage is done to both parties, and to the children.

Few people who have been through a divorce or have witnessed friends and relatives going through a divorce could deny the effects, but in many cases there comes a time when ending the marriage seems the only course to follow. The problems are too numerous, individual needs too diverse, communications too blocked and lines too firmly drawn for productive family life to continue.

A couple in this position should try to be as certain as possible that breaking up the family, with all the conflict, pain and expense involved, really is the *only* and the *best* answer before any steps are taken toward divorce. *If* divorce is the only solution, however, it is not necessary that it be as difficult, traumatic, destructive, and expensive as it frequently is. There is a rational alternative to adversarial divorce in our society. The use of this alternative minimizes the likelihood of the children being used as pawns or weapons, reduces the conflict, cuts the cost (financial as well as emotional), and helps prevent the spouses from emerging as poor battle-scarred veterans of the divorce court. The alternative is called divorce mediation. It is a system which imposes no burden of guilt, no finding of fault. It is a method used to search out a reasonable, equitable and above all, sane solution to divorce dispute.

Divorce Mediation–Definition and Goals

Conflict in family life is an inevitable, frequent and normal occurrence. When individuals have difficulty resolving their conflicts, third party intervention usually helps. Essentially divorce mediation is a method which attempts to resolve difficulties by using a mediator rather than lawyers. Simply, it means helping parties arrive at an agreement through mediation. It is a method whereby people with family problems can benefit from third party intervention. Divorce mediation lessens the possibility of serious harm. Under the old system, two lawyers place the parties in direct confrontation which, as we have seen, often results in escalating difficulties and sometimes permanent damage to the entire family. Divorce mediation never pits one party against another.

A major goal of divorce mediation is to help the couple become rational and responsible enough to co-operate towards making compromises which are acceptable to both people. Voluntary settlements, worked out by the spouses on both an emotional level as well as an intellectual one, are not only more humane than those forced by litigation, but they are also more practical. Mutual agreement means that neither party is the "loser" and that neither has been taken advantage of. Eliminating blame also lessens the possibility of the revenge factor erupting later and leading to prolonged legal battles. Results of research studies are both convincing and encouraging. In practically all of the follow-up studies where couples used divorce mediation, it was found that families were resolving their difficulties in a more positive way. (See Chapter XI.)

Divorce mediation is a therapeutic process through which the counselor provides an atmosphere in which the marital pair is free to bring out and examine openly their pain and their disappointments with regard to their own and their spouse's failure to fulfil expectations. This is frequently a revelation. Many people seem totally unaware of what their spouse expects of marriage.

Divorce mediation is designed to help clients gain enough insight into their marital and family problems as to have a realistic idea of their severity and the possibilities for change. Divorce mediation aims to support the clients by drawing on their own strength to make decisions and accept the responsibilities needed to make their marriage work or, if necessary, dissolve it in the best way possible.

Divorce mediation makes the family the central focus. The family is seen as a social system and, like all systems, each part reflects another part. It is therefore important to take into account *all* of the family members involved in the dispute. *All* of the family members may be only the immediate family or may include other relatives such as step-parents, aunts, uncles and grandparents in particular.

Why all these other family members? Meyer Elkin, writing in an editorial for the *Conciliation Courts Review*, stressed with great sensitivity the importance of grandparents in the divorcing process:

"Grandparents of divorce, like children of divorce, have hardly any legal rights and are voiceless. We have not focused enough attention on the part that grandparents can offer in the lives of their grandchildren during and after the wrenching experience we call divorce. Love comes in many shades. The love of a grandparent for the grandchild is something very special. It is a love that connects the child with the deeper roots parents provide."[5]

Elkin goes on to say, "Reasonable visitation should apply to grandparents just as it applies to parents. Just as we say parents are forever and families are forever, grandparents are also forever and should be acknowledged and recognized as such in the divorce process."[6]

Lawyers, friends and teachers, if considered important to the dispute, may also be involved in the mediation. For example, a teacher can tell a great deal about the child from his or her behavior. Friends and confidants can also shed light on the situation. Lawyers, who are often the first people involved following the decision, can be invaluable in helping the family.

In *Mirages of Marriage*, the authors, William Lederer and Don Jackson, put it this way:

"The systems concept helps explain much of the previously mysterious behavior which results whenever two or more human beings relate to one another. We now know that the family is a unit in which all individuals have an important influence, whether they like it or not and whether they know it or not. The family is an interacting communications network in which every member from the day-old baby to the seventy-year-old grandmother influences the nature of the entire system and in turn is influenced by it. For example, if someone in the family feels ill, another member may function more effectively than he usually does. The system tends, by nature, to keep itself in balance. An unusual action by one member invariably results in a compensating reaction by another member. If mother hates to take Sunday drives but hides this feeling from her husband, the message is nevertheless somehow broadcast throughout the family communications network, and it may be Johnny, the four-year-old, who becomes carsick and ruins the Sunday drive."[7]

What makes divorce mediation different from other forms of therapy is that it focuses on the relationships between family members rather than concentrating on one particular person. Divorce mediation focuses on what is happening in the present rather than dredging up old problems. The manner in which the family uses divorce mediation depends upon how easily it can adapt to change. Timing is an important consideration. Studies have shown that the earlier the family is involved in divorce mediation, the less chance there is of getting caught up in the adversary system. It is important to reach families before problems become thoroughly internalized so that divorce mediation may serve a critical preventative function. When the family is highly motivated to work on their problems, and there is a commitment from all involved, especially lawyers who may have been brought in, the likelihood of resolving the conflict becomes greater.

The human ramifications of divorce are too complex to be dealt with by a single profession such as law, social work, or psychiatry. Co-operative effort between law and the behavioral sciences would result in less fragmentation and a more comprehensive and enduring service to families undergoing breakdown.

Divorce will continue to exist. Conflict between spouses will continue to exist, but it is not necessary to drive this conflict into destructive and expensive channels. Solutions need not be *imposed* by one side or the other through the use of legal methods, deception or cleverness. The adversary system often breeds conflict. Divorce mediation, on the other hand, deals only with resolving family problems in a constructive manner.

No one "wins" when using divorce mediation. Nonetheless, everyone benefits. Parents, children, lawyers, judges, the system and society will all gain when co-operative methods are used instead of destructive confrontation.

Divorce mediation does not offer a panacea to end or reduce

divorce. İt describes a method of minimizing the damage. Divorce alone creates sufficient emotional trauma without the scourge of legal battles.

Divorce mediation is not, of course, for everyone. Doubtless, contested divorce in all its guises will stay with us and be used by those couples who are unable or unwilling to dissolve their marriages in any other manner. These are marriages whose rational dissolution is impossible–marriages which will end in the traditional way with custody being awarded in the traditional way. In some cases it may be a valuable experience. The adversary system must be made available to those people who are unable to settle their disputes otherwise. Unfortunately, this system of pitting one party against the other is too often the court of *first* resort rather than the court of *last* resort.

The most extreme solution should be the last solution to be tried, not the first. We will always need a legal structure that allows people to "have their day in court" when no other method satisfies them. Now, however, there is an alternative for those who choose it. Divorce mediation shows quite conclusively that destructive confrontation is not necessary for the vast majority of divorcing couples.

The odds? They significantly improve with desire and understanding. A closer look at how the adversary system developed and how divorce mediation works by comparison should prove convincing that divorce mediation is worth trying–*first*.

Chapter Two

THE LEGACY OF THE ADVERSARIAL SYSTEM: ITS LOGIC AND DEVELOPMENT

Enlightened members of the legal profession are fully aware that current legal attitudes in North America toward divorce, based as they are on the venerable ecclesiastical notion of fault, are socially irrelevant and psychologically dangerous. Both the social irrelevance and the psychological dangers of the adversary system have been proven in numerous scientific and sociological studies. The professional literature is a testimony in favor of change, but divorce legislation is devilishly slow to catch up. Several legal alternatives have been offered. These range from simple divorce by registration to no-fault divorce.

An old Asiatic curse: May you have a lawsuit in which you know you are right!

It is necessary to investigate the evolution of divorce law in order to understand the adversarial system. In all cultures and religions the definition, method or ability to divorce is based on the concept of marriage. For example, in some African tribal groups, divorce, or the dissolution of the marriage Ćontract, can be accomplished simply by returning the wife to her family together with the dowry received when the marriage took place. In such a case the dissolution of marriage is usually the prerogative of the husband and the husband only. This male prerogative also holds true for most who practice the Muslim religion which, according to custom, allows a husband to repudiate a wife at will. The dissolution of marriage among Roman Catholics or Hindus, on the other hand, is extremely difficult because both religions regard marriage as indissoluble.

27

Today's adversarial system in North America may be traced to pre-Reformation England. The Roman Catholic Church, the only church in pre-Reformation England, regarded marriage as a sacrament. It was thus outside the jurisdiction of civil authority and accepted as indissoluble. Marriage is, of course, still a sacrament but today Catholics can obtain a civil divorce and in some cases may seek a church annulment.

In pre-Reformation England a divorce *a vinculo* (the absolute dissolution of marriage) was not possible within the confines of the ecclesiastical courts that had sole jurisdiction over such matters. Physical separation, *a mensa et thoro*, (without the freedom to remarry) was permissible in extraordinary cases where adultery or extreme cruelty could be proven. Unless such fault could be established, however, not even separation was conceivable.

These were the laws, but history suggests and literature of the period confirms, that the indissoluble quality of marriage did not necessarily affect the morals or mores of the people. Little is known about the common people of the period because little was written about them during the Middle Ages. Life among the nobles is, however, well documented by both historians and writers. Tales of adultery abound in both oral and written literature. Chaucer and Boccaccio's stories suggest that forgiveness could easily be purchased from a corrupt clergy. The bastard sons of nobles were often ruled the rightful heirs to fortunes and the cuckolded husband was a source of fourteenth century humor. Marriage may have been indissoluble but it did not seem to demand fidelity. The "purchase" of forgiveness reached its height during the Great Schism when the Papacy was divided between Avignon and Rome. England recognized the Roman Pope Urban VI while the French recognized the Avignon Papacy led by Clement VII. Confusion reigned supreme. Marriages blessed by one Pope were held invalid by the other. The excesses of the clergy during this period led directly to the Reformation. One can assume that the lusty Wife of Bath was neither exceptional nor unusual.

After the Reformation, ecclesiastical courts similar to those of the Roman Catholic Church were maintained by the Church of England. These too regarded marriage as an indissoluble sacrament. Still, the rules were more flexible for the rich.

By the seventeenth century, life in England was more secularized and it was possible for a wealthy man (rarely a woman) to obtain a divorce *a vinculo*. In order to do so, a man would first have to obtain an ecclesiastical order of separation based on adultery and then his wife's lover would have to be successfully prosecuted. Once these requirements were met, the divorce decree was granted by Parliament: a civil divorce by legislative authority.

In North America no Church of England ecclesiastical courts were established in the British colonies because the population was largely sectarian Protestant and did not admit the validity of laws and procedures based on Catholicism. In New France, prior to 1763 when the last of the French colonies (Quebec) was ceded to England at the end of the French and Indian War, and in the territory colonized by Spain (Mexico and what is now the southwestern United States) the legal foundations were based on Catholic law.

Because the Protestant sects were to some degree iconoclastic, they held that marriage was a civil matter. The common law courts of the British colonies had not inherited a tradition of divorce law from the mother country where it was considered a religious matter. Colonial legislatures and governors were left to deal with the problem of divorce in somewhat the same fashion as England. The religious attitude to divorce in the New World made legislative divorce relatively easy to obtain. Still, the concept of establishing fault was retained and this concept became the basis for divorce proceedings.

Once the American Revolution was over, it was left to individual state legislatures to decide grounds for divorce. Different states were founded by different groups. Louisiana had, for example, been primarily settled by the French, California by the Spanish and the New England states by various Protestant sects. The westward movement diluted the founding groups, but traditional attitudes could often be found in legal statutes.

The variance was further complicated by the fact that some state legislatures came to accept the idea of English ecclesiastical courts, while others did not. Today, state laws vary widely, but one common factor remains to tie them all together: *fault* is the foundation for divorce procedures.

As the nineteenth century drew to a close and the United States and Canada entered a new century, divorce laws gradually began to change. The list of grounds was expanded beyond adultery and physical cruelty. Court orders for alimony, property division and child support and custody began to appear. All of these were subject to the assignment of fault on the part of one of the spouses. Again, individual states and provinces differed in degree, but all were the same in essence.

Today, there has been considerable agitation by law reformers to change the system, although some local authorities still do establish a residence requirement that must be fulfilled and allegations in the form of affidavits by the "innocent" plaintiff must be filed and then proven. If they are proven then the other spouse is the "guilty" defendant. But the purpose of the proceeding is still to find fault. There remain a few justifications which have not progressed far beyond the religious idea that divorce is a sin connected with the punishable offenses of adultery and physical cruelty. Divorce in contemporary society has to do with pleading a prepared case before a judge. Fault is removed from the grounds for divorce but remains for determining which parent is more suitable, with one being awarded custody, and the other visitation rights. The outcome of the case does not depend upon an analysis of the inner family problems that cause the break-up.

To understand the significant attempts to reform divorce legislation in the English-speaking world we must return to England. In 1966, the Archbishop of Canterbury's Group recommended that the *irretrievable breakdown of a marriage* should be the *only* basis for divorce. The Group added that an investigation should be carried out by the court to determine if the breakdown is actually irretrievable. This was a gesture in the right direction, but a conservative English Parliament hamstrung the recommendations of the report when it issued the Divorce Act of 1969. The Act stated that irretrievable breakdown should in fact be the sole cause, but evidence of adultery, cruelty, desertion, or living apart was necessary. Fault still had to be proven.

While living apart is the only grounds for no-fault divorce, there may still be complications. If adultery may be argued to be an effect of living apart, then evidence of adultery could still be introduced. The Act does have one positive benefit. It recommends attempts at reconciliation to the extent that divorce proceedings may be halted while they are in process.

Similar more liberal programs have been suggested in the United States, but to date there is no federal law dealing with divorce. In 1972 a Uniform Marriage and Divorce Act was drafted by the National Conference of Commissioners on Uniform State Laws. It advocated that an "irretrievably broken" marriage be the single cause for divorce. The Act was denied by the American Bar Association. Lawyers seemed reluctant to liberalize the Act as it would lessen the legal thrust of the adversary system. Sweeping reforms have, nevertheless, been carried out in a number of states. California, Michigan and Florida have all adopted no-fault statutes in a special category. In essence, the statutes utilized the idea of living apart and having irreconcilable differences as significant grounds for divorce.

The existence of the no-fault statute does not prevent people from fighting over issues other than property and money. There has been a marked increase in custody disputes which still use a fault basis even though it is not included in the statute. The parties in custody disputes still attempt to prove their worth as parents by showing how the other parent is unfit. This kind of system uses the same tactics and mechanisms that the previous fault-based system of divorce did.

The aforementioned reforms are considerably more far-reaching than the English Divorce Act of 1969, but in practice the idea of no-fault divorce is extremely difficult to define. The specter of the adversary system continues to haunt us.

In 1968, Canada passed a Federal Divorce Act aimed at

clearing clutter and inequality surrounding divorce law. The Act encouraged couples to seek marriage counseling and broadened the grounds of divorce into the area of marital breakdown. Unfortunately, the Act continued to stress the assignment of fault. Administration of the details–custody, maintenance, property settlement and so on–was left to the individual provinces. This led to some very interesting changes in provincial divorce law. In Ontario, for instance, marital property is now subject to a 50 percent division between spouses. Under ideal circumstances this is a victory for thousands of women who, before changes in the law, might have been left penniless and unable to earn a living when their marriages broke up. This change in the law recognized the contribution of the homemaker to the couple's accumulated property.

Enlightened members of the legal profession are fully aware that current legal attitudes in North America toward divorce, based as they are on the venerable ecclesiastical notion of fault, are socially irrelevant and psychologically dangerous. Both the social irrelevance and the psychological dangers of the adversary system have been proven in numerous scientific and sociological studies. The professional literature is a testimony in favor of change, but divorce legislation is devilishly slow to catch up. Several legal alternatives have been offered. These range from simple divorce by registration to no-fault divorce. As alternatives these should be examined.

The concept of divorce by registration does not appear feasible since it might create an epidemic. Instantaneous divorce would serve as an outlet for hasty judgement and, in any event, still leaves the questions of custody and property division.

No-fault divorce, on the other hand, sounds at the outset like a sane solution. Ideally, it would enable couples to dissolve a dead marriage without having to prove innocence or guilt. Unfortunately, no-fault divorce as it currently exists has not been given the unique legal status it deserves. Rather than enacting new no-fault divorce laws the concept has been appended to existing, fault-based legislation. The legal option of fault-finding is still alarmingly real, particularly when no-fault divorce is carried out by lawyers who have a preference for adversarial action.

To their friends, the marriage of Mr. and Mrs. Morrow was as perfect as a modern marriage could be. They were financially comfortable, though not wealthy. They were both intelligent and committed to each other. Mr. Morrow was a successful draftsman who worked on several major corporate projects. Mrs. Morrow was a skilled executive secretary in a brokerage house. Between them they earned close to thirty-five thousand dollars annually. Their joint income was sufficient to support a suburban townhouse, an Oldsmobile and a Volkswagen and a private education for their two children. They had problems, of course, but the couple was secure about their ability to solve them.

At first both were interested in succeeding in their careers for the benefit of the family as a whole, but as competition grew heavier and their individual careers grew more demanding, they gradually began to grow apart. They developed separate goals, separate friends. As a result these intelligent people sought relief in mutual understanding. They acknowledged the fact that each of them had separate needs to fulfil. Their communal life with the children began to disintegrate. Lessons were found for the children to attend and summer camps were organized.

Sexually, Mr. and Mrs. Morrow had a satisfactory relationship and genuinely liked and respected one another. Then, at forty-five and forty respectively, a certain boredom set in. The boredom alternated with frenzied attempts to recapture the old urgency–the romance had disappeared. Various experiments were tried. These included separate vacations, marital counseling sessions, and even individual psychotherapy. But important communication between them had all but ceased. The only logical alternative, it seemed, was a friendly divorce in which no one would be unduly damaged, especially the children. Separately, they consulted their surprised friends for the names of lawyers who might help.

An "up front" decision was reached, in the form of "open

marriage." During this period the Morrows maintained a façade of understanding. "Did you have a good time last night, dear? Your date looked interesting."

Separate relationships accelerated and as they became more superficial they became less "meaningful." The children began to show the strain. This was clear from the classroom behavior of their thirteen-year-old daughter Alice. Alice's teacher noted the child's dramatic shift of mood. She had become practically non-communicative, shied away from her friends and seemed lonely and unhappy. The school psychologist, after assessing Alice, reported that she was reacting to an unhappy home situation. In confidence, the child had told the psychologist that she thought *she* was responsible for her parents' inability to get along. Alice's teacher summoned the Morrows to school to discuss Alice's behavioral change. The outcome seemed inevitable.

People in the midst of divorce, no matter how simple it is meant to be, are seldom given to rational actions. While undergoing marital discord, they are under a great deal of stress and do not function as they might under normal conditions. They may be impulsive, aggressive, or turn inward and become withdrawn and moody. The symptoms are really not very different from those produced by any major crisis people experience during their lifetimes. The range of emotional responses varies from individual to individual.

In this case, Mrs. Morrow's lawyer suggested that she sue for custody and a liberal maintenance settlement. Mr. Morrow's lawyer suggested that he recover a major portion of the property. The Morrows had entered the downward spiral of destructive conflict inherent in the adversary system. From this point on they themselves would have to assume the role of adversaries. The chances of any co-operative effort were lessened as each threat and counter-threat built up through lawyers' letters and affidavits.

This inherent aspect, as discussed by Judge Lois Forer who has years of experience with family, civil and criminal law, criticizes Canon 7 of the Code of Professional Responsibility, saying, "A lawyer is licensed by the government and is under sworn duty to uphold and defend the law and the Constitution of the United States, despite the license and the oath. The role of the lawyer is by definition and by law amoral. He must press the position of his client even though it is contrary to the public good, popular opinion and widely accepted standards of behavior. Canon 7, promulgated by the American Bar Association, declares in part 'The duty of a lawyer, both to his client and to the legal system is to represent his client zealously within the bounds of the law.' . . . If the client wishes to sue or contest a claim, the lawyer must either zealously pursue his client's interest or withdraw from the case."[1] And, if he does withdraw, there are no doubt others standing by who will gladly take it on. But many lawyers do refuse to accept a case where they feel the motivation and nature of the situation is inappropriate or even harmful to the family.

Mr. Morrow would have quite frankly stated that he wasn't particularly angry with anyone and that he only wanted to end a dead relationship. When his lawyer contacted him, he was not surprised, but the reason given for the requested meeting did give him a shock. Mrs. Morrow, it seemed, had just filed an affidavit swearing to the occurrence of an incident proving mental cruelty, as grounds for divorce. The affidavit, his lawyer explained, was a *public record* that might be used in court. Mr. Morrow simply could not believe his ears when he heard the affidavit. "My husband stood in front of me naked, all the while telling me how he wanted to sleep with my friend, Susan, and what he would do with her." Mr. Morrow was shocked, angry, hurt and ready to retaliate with relatively little prompting from his counsel. He tried to recall the circumstances and his frank response was, "Well, I probably did say that I found Susan sexually attractive, but I never meant it in the way she said I did."
Numerous conflicting stories were repeated to them by mutual friends, so each soon saw that confidences had been betrayed. Long-time intimate friends were caught up in the struggle. In many cases they did not wish to be further involved and so withdrew. To make matters worse, the children, the

couple's parents and in-laws began taking sides. What had been a close network of family and friends deteriorated and left the couple isolated. Mr. Morrow retaliated and incorporated his own bad feelings about the breakdown of the marriage and the humiliating damage caused by the details revealed in his wife's affidavit by filing his own affidavit. He swore that Mrs. Morrow was an unfit mother and that she mistreated the children, leaving them alone and exposing them to her own sexual misconduct.

Both affidavits sworn out by the Morrows were public documents. They could not be retracted. In better moods, Mrs. Morrow would admit that during the marriage they had both discussed their desire for other partners, while for his part, Mr. Morrow would admit that his wife was not an unfit mother and that the one time she left the kids alone had been years ago when she went to borrow something from a neighbor. Nevertheless, at this point in their escalating battle, retaliation was the order of the day. On the advice of her lawyer Mrs.Morrow moved out of their bedroom and slept on the studio couch in the den. When I asked her about this, she said the lawyer advised that this was an effective technique that might get her husband to move out of the house. She was in fact instructed to reject her husband in a variety of ways. Interestingly, she was not entirely convinced that this was the proper behavior.

Mr. Morrow's reaction was predictable. He would stay late at the office and he began to drink excessively. He sought other female companionship to build up his damaged ego. Letters were sent back and forth between family members. The in-laws, who had always been friendly, took definite sides and supported their respective children. The children were told by each parent that the other parent was responsible for the marital breakdown.

The parents became extremely competitive and vied for the love and support of their children. They were no longer in control of the children as they found themselves being too liberal in an effort to remain close. Expensive presents, trips, and the like were provided to excess. The youngsters soon became confused, sad and eventually their behavior was unacceptable and anti-social. Each parent blamed the other for the children's actions. Each began to openly demean and undermine the other in front of the children. This destructive scenario repeated itself on an escalating basis, so it was inevitable that what would follow would be a bitter and extensive contested divorce.

The affidavits stood. Mrs. Morrow's psychiatrist was called, and Mr. Morrow followed suit. Each was a high-priced advocate for his client.

At this point in the Morrows' story it is appropriate to discuss the role of the so-called "expert witness." The role of the "expert witness" is, in fact, contradictory. Far from being an impartial witness in possession of specialized factual information, the expert witness is present only to promote his patient's case. The expert witness and the lawyer form a team. The other side, of course, has its own team. Neither one of the expert witnesses–in this case the psychiatrists–had ever interviewed the other spouse. Each, however, made claims and counterclaims about the suitability of his patient and the unsuitability of the other spouse. It is anti-ethical to present information in this way since it serves only as a catalyst to further divide the parents. How can one expect agreements and co-operation when using this method? Not only does the legalese of the affidavits drive the parties apart, but psychiatric language fuels the process.

During the course of the Morrows' divorce, friends, relatives and even the couple's children were interrogated and cross-examined. The children's grandparents, who had once had an excellent relationship, stopped speaking to each other. The entire network of relationships that had been built up around the marriage was shattered. Everyone took sides.

It is unfortunate to note that these kinds of cases end up going back to court even after the judge has ruled on the case itself. This is not surprising since the language used in this process itself contributes to the unresolved nature of the litigation. For example, the fact that custody is awarded to the "winner" as if the child or children were a prize, is discouraging.

What about the loser? What happens to the children? The loser is labeled the visiting parent. If the visiting parent is lucky, some kind of "access" to the children will be agreed to. It *is* implied, of course, that the loser was "at fault." After all, this is what the adversary system is about.

The couple being divorced are not the only losers. Children and in-laws are not asking for a divorce and yet, in reality, they are cut off and divorced from close relationships. The consequences of the kind of case described above is sometimes termed "the revolving courtroom door" situation. Years after the court decision, families still find themselves going back to court and fighting over other legal issues.

The direct result of the Morrows' bitter struggle was that Mr. Morrow lost his children, Mrs. Morrow was financially ruined, both their careers suffered and their children required extended therapy. Each lost a great many friends. Nonetheless, the lawyers, the courts and the system were satisfied. There were winners and losers! The scenario of this actual case is unfortunately all too common. Such a scenario is the most dismal and tawdry symptom of what has been called adversarial divorce, which often uses destructive confrontation as its method.

Responsible members of the legal profession freely admit that the adversary system, including the so-called uncontested kind of divorce, is not functioning to anyone's benefit save the unscrupulous lawyer who makes a substantial living from destructive conflict. Such lawyers are few in number, but significant nonetheless.

The role played by some lawyers often worsens the relationship between spouses; that this would have an adverse impact on children seems obvious.

Robert Weiss points out an adverse effect relating to the adversarial system:

"It is possible for lawyers to negotiate too hard. In pursuit of the best possible agreement for their clients, some lawyers seem to worsen the post-marital relationship of their client and the client's spouse. They may, for example, actively discourage a client from talking with his or her spouse for fear that the client wil inadvertently weaken his or her negotiating position, or will, in thoughtless generosity, make concessions without obtaining anything in return. Or, they may take positions more extreme than their client desires in order eventually to achieve an advantageous compromise, but by so doing anger the client's spouse and further alienate the spouse from the client. Some separated individuals reported that until negotiations were at an end, their relationship with their spouse became progressively worse."[2]

The role of the divorce attorney as an adversary is described by Herbert Glieberman in his recent book, *Confessions of a Divorce Lawyer.*

"There's only one rule on divorce settlement: If you represent the wife, get as much as possible; if you represent the husband, give away as little as possible." The author goes on to say, "Now, as I walk through the outer door of my office heading for the courtroom, I know that I'm walking to a case where there will be no compromises, no conciliations, no good feelings to balance the bad. This will be an all-out confrontation, a real tooth and nail fight. I'll love it. Now, finally we're here. And it's a real circus. The other side has two accountants, a tax lawyer, three expert witnesses and a defendant; our side has one accountant, a comptroller, no tax lawyers because I've become expert at that, and seven expert witnesses."[3]

Lawyers are trained to win. There is no intention here to attack the legal profession as a whole because there are many fine lawyers who are themselves trapped within the adversary system. "Legal training is calculated to promote close reasoning and argumentation in favor of a partisan interest; in short, to develop the art of advocacy."[4] The lawyer, as an advocate, is required to represent or advocate solely the interest of his client. He cannot represent both parties, as is commonly supposed. The lawyer represents his client within the "light of his professional judgement." The client's interest is always viewed as being in opposition to the interests of the other party. The lawyer cannot and does not regard the parties as having a common problem which he or she will help resolve.

The canons of professional ethics effectively prohibit a

lawyer from active collaboration with the opposing side against the interests of his own client, thereby making it more difficult to effect a real solution to the dispute between the parties. Moreover, some lawyers perceive reconciliation as a threat to the partisan advocacy which they offer to their clientele. Reconciliation can be a costly affair for the attorney. Paul Conway puts it this way: ". . . He has a Hobson's Choice between trying to save the marriage and losing the legal fees if he is successful, or unsuccessfully attempting to save the marriage and again losing fees, because he cannot ethically represent either of the parties."[5]

When a lawyer recognizes the fact that he is dealing with emotional rather than strictly legal issues and wishes to help the client come to grips with the real problems involved, he is stymied in attempts to counsel the client because of his traditional role and legal training. Even when the lawyer is open to functioning in a new role, the client tends to see him as an advocate.

As for the parties themselves, the use of the adversary system might be seen as an abdication of their responsibility to each other and to their children. After all, since a court order can't be dealt with, it is often passed off with a shrug—a decree from on high that has little to do with reality. "Christ, this alimony is killing me, but she had a smart lawyer!" or, "The bastard has the kids half the summer, I can't believe that judge!" are both common responses.

Given the present adversarial system and the role of the lawyer in implementing it, Susan Gettleman and Janet Markowitz describe it this way:

"People often feel compelled to find lawyers who are shrewd, politically connected, or famous for their ruthlessness. The public has been conditioned to believe that a good lawyer has to use fraud, and use it well to combat a fraudulent legal system. Given our present system of divorce, good lawyers have to be ruthless on behalf of their clients. The growing hostility of the public toward divorce laws, lawyers, and judges who administer the law is a healthy sign that a basis for change may be at hand. People are becoming justifiably suspicious of the 'high priests of the law, who are supposed to be objective, professional and competent'."[6]

These and many more commentaries bear witness to the fact that the system is tottering and that needed reform is long overdue. The fact is recognized by an ever-growing number of lawyers and judges.

Even so, some of the blame must be placed on the choices made by individuals in the first instance. When you want groceries you don't go to a furniture store. When you need help with an intense problem involving human relations a lawyer may not be the most desirable first stop. This is where divorce mediation comes in–it is the available alternative first stop. The consequences of traditional divorce are disastrous. Surely it is worth the time to explore the alternative: divorce mediation.

Chapter Three

EVOLUTION OF DIVORCE MEDIATION

In North America, court-based conciliation (or mediation) programs have grown out of the frustrating experiences of Family Court judges who daily see couples whom they are unable to help. These couples stand before the bench with their prepared cases and their lawyers; the judge knows that mere decisions on custody, access and maintenance will not really help the individuals in front of him. The formation of conciliation programs has been an attempt to cope with these more important problems.

Mediation is not a new invention thrust on us by the industrialized era. This concept has existed for centuries and is among the oldest ideas of community life. The Beth Din, a Jewish religious court that began thousands of years ago, serves as one example. The Beth Din is part of the modern Israeli legal system, out of which has grown the Jewish Conciliation Board, founded in 1920. In his book, *So Sue Me*, James Yaffe discusses the Board, which perceives itself "'not only as a body that dispenses justice, but even more as a body that tries to make peace among the disputants.' As one judge put it, 'We are not going to attempt to say who is morally or legally justified; we are interested in settling things.' Another judge comments, 'Our religious tradition teaches us that it doesn't matter who is right or wrong. There should be a sense of compassion and forgiveness.' A third judge, about to deliver an extremely conciliatory decision said, 'This may be rough justice, but here it is.' When one of the litigants objects that the justice is a bit too rough, the judge states the mandate of the Board firmly: 'In Jewish law we don't just go by the paragraph; we go beyond it.' The judges pay more than lip service to conciliation–they spend a lot of time trying to achieve it in individual cases.

"Disputes between man and the state are much less common than disputes between men and other men. And in such disputes true justice may be as much involved with the personalities of the disputants, their peculiar standards of morality, their economic and social conditions, their half-conscious motives and half-expressed desires, the lives they will have to go back to after they leave the court, as it is with the specific issues of the case.

"Some people observing the activities of the court are offended by what they consider to be its inconsistency. Some interpret board decisions as symptomatic of 'sloppy thinking.' The charge is absolutely correct. The judges of the court may have small minds–in this respect they are like most of us–but at least consistency is not one of their hobglobins. They recognize instinctively that they are dealing with one of the most malleable, volatile, unpredictable, inconsistent elements ever created–*human nature*. Their mixture of toughness and compassion, pragmatism and idealism seems completely appropriate. The proof of the court's success lies in the results achieved. The judges find people are more willing to believe what you tell them, more willing to grow and change, when they feel they have been approached as people rather than as abstractions whose individual needs must be fitted into the puzzle of a rigid system."[1]

The Jewish arbitration courts consist of an impartial third party group that acts as a community tribunal to solve or mediate disputes without resorting to civil authority.

The process of arbitration and mediation as a fact of community life is not restricted to Jewish culture. Japan, for example, has a population of 120,000,000 people served by 10,000 lawyers. The United States has a population of 220,000,000 people served by 350,000 lawyers.[2] Without question, North America is the most litigation-prone area in the world. Courts in Canada and the United States dispense justice and Japanese courts do fundamentally the same thing. The Japanese, however, have an end in mind that is similar to the end sought by the judges of the Jewish arbitration courts. That end is to restore the harmony which has been shattered by the event of antagonism.On the one hand the end is seen to be "justice," on the other the end is seen to be the restoration of harmony. There is a tremendous difference between these two premises. The Japanese legal system sets out at the beginning to harmonize the views of the antagonists. Anyone who resists such a compromise in Japan is, in the eyes of the judge and Japanese society, apt to be denounced as recalcitrant. The rules are, in a sense, set by the culture. People are expected to play by them.

Since the restoration of harmony is the main theme of Japanese justice, the avoidance of litigation is a high priority. The result is that most disputes are settled by using mediation techniques rather than by going to trial.

China serves as another example of a country where a preference for mediation is evident in the legal system, as pointed out recently by a group of lawyers who visited to observe the family court process. "The Chinese would much rather persuade disputants to resolve their difficulties in a particular way instead of ordering them to accept a given decision. To appreciate the extent to which the legal system as a whole reflects this preference for arbitration, it is worthwhile noting that few civil disputes even reach a formal court. By far the majority of disputes are resolved through the efforts of community mediation organizations or by judicial personnel attached to the court system. The reasons underlying this preference are cultural, historical and philosophical. Mediation has been the primary mode of dispute resolution in China for centuries. It was not introduced by the Communist government, but dates back to the teachings of Confucius. Confucianism is based on the goal of preserving natural harmony in the world and thus requires a dispute resolution mechanism that discourages confrontation and encourages compromise. No one could doubt that mediation meets this requirement far better than adjudication. In preferring mediation, therefore, the Communist government was opting for a method of resolving disputes that was familiar to, and very much accepted by, the broad masses of the Chinese people."[3]

The principle is stated clearly in the Marriage Law of The People's Republic of China (Article 17 . . .)

In the event of either the husband or wife alone insisting upon divorce, it may be granted only when mediation by the district people's government and the judicial organ has failed to bring about reconciliation . . . When one party insists on divorce, the district people's government may try to effect a reconciliation. If such mediation fails, it should, without delay, refer the case to the county or municipal people's court for decision. The district people's government should not attempt to prevent or to obstruct either party from appealing to the county or municipal people's court. In dealing with a divorce case, the county or municipal people's court should, in the first instance, try to bring about a reconciliation between the parties. In case such mediation fails, the court should render a decision without delay.[4]

In North America, court-based conciliation (or mediation) programs have grown out of the frustrating experiences of Family Court judges who daily see couples whom they are unable to help. These couples stand before the bench with their prepared cases and their lawyers; the judge knows that mere decisions on custody, access and maintenance will not really help the individuals in front of him. The formation of conciliation programs has been an attempt to cope with these more important problems.

It has been suggested that one of the reasons for the American Bar Association denial of the Uniform Marriage and Divorce Act was that it made no provision for conciliation as part of divorce procedure as the Canadian and English Acts do. Still, many lawyers are apprehensive regarding a statement in favor of conciliation as they fear it may lead their clients into discussions of getting back together again when in fact their decision has been made to separate. They feel that such a procedure, in the face of a definite decision to separate would make things more difficult for their clients. There seems to be a misunderstanding among some of these lawyers. They interpret conciliation to be an approach to reunite the couple. This concern is legitimate since many lawyers have had experience with marriage counselors who do not practice divorce mediation. These lawyers are unaware that conciliation is a method that helps families to *separate in the least destructive way.* It is also true that some lawyers resist conciliation for other reasons. Obviously, a lawyer would in effect lose a client if the dispute is settled without a long expensive courtroom trial. One can only assume that those lawyers who are more radical and reform-minded and who saw divorce mediation as a viable alternative simply did not have enough clout to see to it that conciliation was included as an integral part of the Uniform Marriage and Divorce Act. Probably the vast number of lawyers reject conciliation because they misunderstand it. Conciliation should be defined and understood.

Essentially, divorce mediation constitutes agreement-oriented counseling by a neutral third party directed at persons whose marriage is near breakdown or has already broken down (i.e. divorced). It is a process, moreover, "by which families are helped to identify and clarify issues between them and are assisted in making agreement on some or all of these issues; especially, but not limited to, disputes over custody and access to children."[5] Finally, it is a service based on the twin assumptions that persons experiencing family problems can benefit from third party intervention; and that conciliation counselor mediation may minimize whatever damage will be done. It is a means of obtaining time for couples to stop and think so that divorce might be contemplated more objectively and so that the option of reconciliation might be explored. Conciliation is not a method that demands the reunification of the couple.

Large scale, court-based conciliation projects have been operating for some time in several North American cities: New

York, Atlanta, Minneapolis, Phoenix, Los Angeles, Edmonton and Toronto, to mention a few.

To a large extent all of these projects have their theoretical base in the Los Angeles County Conciliation Court that was originally started in 1939. Its role is primarily therapeutic. It functions as a department of the Superior Court of Los Angeles and its stated purpose is "to protect the rights of children and to promote the public welfare by preserving, promoting and protecting family life and the institution of matrimony, and to provide means for the reconciliation of spouses and the amicable settlement of family controversies." (California Code, Section 1730).

In California the procedure takes the following form, and to varying degrees this form has become the pattern for most similar projects.

It works this way: a short term series of conciliation meetings is set up. Where reconciliation seems possible a lengthy Marriage Agreement is drawn up that defines the marital disputes and offers possible solutions. Lawyers do have a tendency to be less enthusiastic about these agreements because they are not legally binding and may be dissolved at any time. However, such agreements often have the positive psychological benefits of identifying problems where direct communication has probably been blocked and of seeking joint solutions that may very well be upheld.

Professional counselors were first employed in California in 1954. Between 1954 and 1974, nearly 20,000 families were reconciled. The reconciled disputes involved approximately 35,000 children. Of the group reconciled nearly 25% separated again after one year. There are, however, an average of 45,000 family law petitions filed each year in Los Angeles County. Obviously, the conciliation project is dealing with only a fraction of the total number of problems in the area. Nevertheless, the legislators have responded quite favorably to these positive results and have set up numerous conciliation services throughout the family courts in the State of California. It is interesting to note that even with this good track record the conciliation court services of California have to fight yearly in order to obtain funds to sustain their services.

If the conciliation courts were to deal with the entire case load instead of the percentage now dealt with, staff would have to be increased tenfold and the cost of such an expansion would be prohibitive. Still, even that cost would probably be less than the cost of services which are needed to pick up the pieces.

The experience of the Los Angeles project shows that reconciliation, while it is important for some couples, might better be handled by other social agencies such as public or private family therapists. The project might be made more effective by dealing only with mediated divorce while couples who wish to reconcile could be referred to qualified people outside the project. A second consideration is the case load. The per capita case load is larger than any other on the continent and it illustrates the fact that projects operating on public funds have definite limits. This limitation suggests a need to expand the list of private mediators whose fees would be paid by the individuals using their services. Such private mediators could control the size of their practice and thus extend the attention given to each couple.

Even though the Los Angeles project serves as a model for projects in other cities, the emphasis on reconciliation may vary according to the demand and the experience of each particular location. Meyer Elkin, the past Director of the Family Counseling Services of the Los Angeles Conciliation Court, emphasizes the fact that the court has a broader function than reconciliation. As the purpose of the Court is to serve families, Elkin argues that divorce does not end the family, for the parents remain parents and have continued responsibilities towards the children.[6] *Marital separation and divorce represent a crisis for most spouses and many consider themselves failures as a result. Through conciliation counseling, according to Elkin, a spouse can turn such a crisis into personal growth. So family counseling in the Los Angeles Conciliation Court has both a reconciliation and a conciliation function.*

The findings of conciliators, the procedures involved in conciliation and the emphasis placed on reconciliation by some court-based programs were studied by a Toronto group of which this writer was co-director. The study was intended to establish the need and feasibility of a conciliation project that would be attached to the Toronto Family Court. It involved historical research as well as a series of questionnaires distributed to spouses, lawyers and judges. Those questioned favored a conciliation court whose primary aim would be to help families resolve their disputes with a few sessions and refer long-term counseling to other service agencies. The court would encourage spouses to attend at least one meeting with a conciliator. On the question of reconciliation, however, judges observed that it had very little impact on the problem of divorce.

In the Toronto Family Court conciliation project some preliminary findings are very promising. Approximately 75-80 percent of families who were at the courtroom door ready to proceed with litigation were able to settle their differences following mediation. The approach involves not only the family but lawyers and judges as well. The sessions which are rather brief considering other forms of family counseling, are usually not more than five or six sessions. The results after a one year follow-up revealed that many of these agreements are still in force and that the parties to the dispute were highly satisfied. (This is reviewed in more detail in the final chapter.)

For financial and personal reasons, many people prefer to use clinics when they need medical help while others prefer a private doctor. In my experience as a mediator I find divorcing couples no different. Some people would prefer to go to a mediator in private practice rather than use a court-based, public service. Both systems have advantages. The implicit power of the court is necessary for some couples because it makes them feel that they should settle their differences. Other couples, however, may feel intimidated by the legal implications of the court-based system.

The main difference between court-based conciliation projects and private mediation is that those involved in private mediation are able to choose their own mediator. In some areas private practitioners advertize their services under the heading

Divorce Counseling, while in other areas the Family or Supreme Court furnishes a list of qualified individuals. The independent mediator's fee may range from thirty-five to forty-five dollars an hour. As in the public service, the entire process may require four to six sessions of sixty minutes each.

Another model of private mediation services has been developed by O. J. Coogler, a lawyer with a great deal of experience in family mediation. The approach, which is called Structured Mediation, utilizes the services of mediators and an advisory attorney (who assists both parties) and follows agreed-upon written rules of mediation. The Family Mediation Association located in Atlanta, Georgia has seen over 100 couples since its inception in 1976.[7]

If one chooses a private mediator the cost may appear high, but when private mediation costs are compared to the exorbitant cost of adversarial divorce, they are minimal fees. In order to better understand what is involved, let us compare the cost of mediation with the costs of the traditional adversarial method.

It is true that only a small percentage of cases go on to litigation even with the traditional adversarial system. In fact, close to 90 percent are settled out-of-court. This, unfortunately, does not mean a minimal financial cost. Many cases settled out-of-court have had years of affidavits, letters, consultations and numerous court hearings. When one realizes that the lawyer's rate of anywhere from $50.00 to $100.00 per hour is applied to telephone calls, letter writing, court appearances, meetings with friends, relatives, and expert witnesses–all in preparation for the court hearing–it is no wonder that families are driven further and further into debt. Moreover, in some states lawyers receive a percentage of the final settlement, known as a "contingency fee."

Naturally, those cases that go on to litigation face another added financial burden as the court costs are roughly $800.00 to $1000.00 per day for each side. It is important to note that these costs are comparable in both the United States and Canada. How much "justice" can people afford with this kind of system? It is beyond imagination that people who are undergoing a psychologically devastating experience can cope with catastrophic legal and court fees. For many men there is added insult in that they have to pay their wives' lawyers who in effect are running up the costs of their case. If this weren't enough, it is a well-known fact that the most litigious cases keep coming back for more litigation even after the courts have made decisions. Added to lawyers' fees and court costs are the costs of expert witnesses. They charge not only for consultations with the client and lawyer, but also for time spent in court.

It is not surprising that some fathers who could not afford the legal fees leave the area in which they were living and disengage completely from their children, rather than face financial ruin.

This harmful approach to divorce also contributes to the growing number of spouses defaulting on maintenance and support orders. For example a study of maintenance orders in Wisconsin showed an alarming 60 percent of spouses did not fully discharge their payments, while 42 percent didn't make any payments at all.[8] A study of the Law Reform Commission in Canada revealed that the Ontario Provincial Courts (Family Division) showed only 55 percent of support payments had been fully discharged.[9]

There are, of course, legal clinics and legal aid coverage for the destitute. It has been the experience of many in the field of mediation that legal aid cases can go on indefinitely in the courts because of the very fact that lawyers are guaranteed payment under the system. It is paradoxical that those who cannot afford legal fees are able to proceed indefinitely in the adversary system while those who can afford fees are stripped of their assets in a relatively short period of time. I can recall one case where the family were legal aid recipients. When I asked the lawyer to encourage his client in the process of divorce mediation regarding an access situation, the lawyer made it clear that he did not approve of mediation and that after all, society was paying him for this case so why should I be concerned. He went on to explain that the purpose of legal aid was to give people their day in court. His attitude was not typical of all lawyers–not even of all lawyers who take legal aid clients–but it points to the fact that when the profit motive is involved and applied to family law, we must be careful that a needed and well-designed social instrument such as legal aid is not used for the wrong motives. It seems uncanny that in a culture that prizes individual freedom and justice, the reverse often occurs when the mechanism that provides that freedom and justice is applied to the basic institution of our society–the family.

Chapter Four

ADVERSARIAL DIVORCE AND ITS EFFECTS ON THE FAMILY

Unhappily, the adversarial system may contribute to the attitude that the child or children are pawns–prizes who go to the winner. Parents, like it or not, are models for their children. Children of divorce react in a variety of ways, but often those ways reflect the actions of the parents. Like a mirror, the various emotional phases of the divorce may be seen in the actions of the children.

As the number of divorces approaches epidemic proportions, it becomes increasingly important that we understand the effects of divorce on the family. Earlier it was pointed out that three-quarters of divorces involve children and that all divorces affect the total family and friendship networks. The consequences of divorce, whether positive or negative, reach out beyond the couple–they touch and have a lasting influence on children, grandparents, siblings and the friends of each spouse.

It is unfortunate to note that little research looks at the effects of divorce on the family. Instead there are conflicting reports on divorce and its impact on children. The fact that all family members are in some way involved in the divorce process has escaped both clinicians and researchers. To deny the fact that family members are intimately involved and are interdependent is both irresponsible and dangerous. A change in one part of the family results in a change throughout the family. In a research study investigating relationships between young married couples and their parents, the findings consistently indicated that there was a good deal of interaction and help between the couples.[1] In fact, the most usual source of help in all areas of family life for the young married couples was parents first and parents-in-law second. This family "support system" was most evident in times of crisis. Young married couples were also found to seek out their parents and in-laws for emotional support and as confidants. In essence, the study, coupled with several other research undertakings, has dispelled the myth of the isolated nuclear family. The extended family system does still exist, albeit in a slightly different form.

This knowledge is particularly disconcerting when one looks at the current research on divorce. This research isolates the child as if he or she were separate and apart from other family members. This, quite naturally, makes it extremely difficult to gain any insights on the total family from the results of the studies. The picture that emerges is a confusing array of conflicting theories and polarized views as to the effects of divorce on children.

In their book, *The Disposable Parent*, authors Roman and Haddad discuss the prevalent myth that the children of divorce are more likely to be delinquent, sexually maladjusted, underachieving and emotionally unstable than children of intact families.[2] This misconception, or view, of the children of divorce has been put forward by a number of authors. The child is described as a victim of his parents' poor character or, at best, mental illness, and this view seems to relegate the child to a life of failure. Given the commonness of this myth, we might remember Joseph Epstein's statement in *Divorced in America* that "In the realm of manners and morals, one day's advanced thought often turns out to be the next day's retrograde opinion."[3] When a child is in trouble, teachers, social workers and psychologists want to find reasons. If the child is from a home that has experienced marriage breakdown the breakdown may be offered as the reason. The view is unsubstantiated, however, as we shall see.

At the other end of the spectrum is the rather smug view that divorce is an opportunity for growth and change. Though doubtless well-meaning, this view does nothing more than promote the general idea that divorce is a necessary growing experience for the self-actualizing individual and a fashionable "thing to do." This view presents divorce as a necessity for the "growing person," something to be fitted in between courses on macramé and pottery. Though freedom undoubtedly is the result in some divorces, such generalized thinking often leads to irresponsible and erratic behavior. This outlook also promulgates the theory that the child is resilient and will bounce back without any negative effect. Certainly, some marriages need to be dissolved for the health of family members, not the least of whom are the children. The fact remains, however, that the actual consequences of adversarial divorce are not measured by statistics or rhetoric. In the majority of cases such divorces create a great deal of conflict, pain and loss for the couple, the children and all other involved family and friends.

Although the divorcing experience is not always "for the worse," it can be stated with assurance that even when it is for "the better," difficult problems related to life changes occur for family members. Those changes include the obvious: changes in living arrangements, finances, child care, social relationships, job status. In essence, they add up to total re-adjustment. In studies of psychological and physical crises, the findings revealed that divorce and separation rank second and third on the scale of seriousness behind the adjustment to death of the spouse.[4]

Those studies which have been done clearly indicate that families undergoing separation are a potentially high risk. The way in which the family members, especially the separating couple, handle the divorcing process appears to be the most important indicator of whether or not there will be any damaging effects following the divorce.

Divorce "can be perceived as a threat, as a loss, or as a challenge; in each situation the response will differ in terms of perception; thus a threat to basic needs or integrity leads to a response of depression; and a challenge will lead to the mobilization of new modes of problem-solving. It is evident that divorce contains elements of all three types of responses."[5]

When one considers the degree of emotion and psychological investment that is put into a marriage, it is not difficult to understand some of the irrational behavior that takes place during the breakup of the family. In my practice I have heard divorcing couples describe the process as a form of death. The symptoms they describe are not unlike the mourning process. Adelaide Ferguson describes these various emotional stages as (1) a denial of what is happening; (2) depression and a feeling that everything is hopeless (loneliness and sadness, it should be noted, are important parts of depression); (3) anger–this phase often takes people by surprise, particularly those who have not found it easy to identify and express their own anger in the past. During this phase, one of the partners may relate their bewilderment at how this breakdown has occurred when there was never any previous complaint or fighting between them. It is almost as if, rather than directly confronting each other with their unhappiness, the couple, or at least one of them, becomes vulnerable and begins complaining to a third party, often the lawyer. During this phase of anger, when one member is particularly weakened by the process, lawyers become involved and this can encourage the parties to direct their anger through the legitimate means of the adversarial system. Finally, during the fourth stage, called bargaining, the partners try to make deals with one another and, in most cases, they begin to accept and deal with the inevitability of the divorce.[6]

Most researchers and clinicians tend to describe two patterns that are revealed in the divorcing process. Westman and Cline describe the process in this way: "(1) Parent-centered–that is, the two adults are too involved in their conflicts to see the effect it has on the children. It usually involves one discrediting the other. (2) Child-centered–in this situation, the affected children manipulate the parents to perpetuate continued conflict or to promote re-uniting of them."[7] Here, for example, is a letter written by a divorced father to his son who remains in the mother's custody. The father is bitter enough about the marriage breakup to be made blind to the effects his harmful words will have on the boy. The man's feelings are obvious to an objective third party, however.

> *Dear Mark:*
>
> *Well, we finally made it. Your brother Bill and I have been lying on the beach here in sunny California. Only one thing is missing and that's you, big fella! If mom wasn't so mean and trying her best to keep us apart, you'd be here with us. Bill mentioned to me when we were leaving Disneyland the other night, how sad it made him feel that you couldn't be with us.*
>
> *When we come back, I'm going to ask my lawyer if he can help me to get you to come and live with us. I know it will be difficult, but it's the only way that we can stop your mom from keeping us apart. With all the legal bills she had made me pay, it's really going to be hard on Bill and I, but your wonderful grandmother has offered to lend me $2000.00 to help pay the legal bill. I hope your mother knows what she is doing to us, and that some day soon we will win out and she will know what it's like to suffer the way we are now. The next time you see the shrink, make sure you tell him how unhappy you are, and how much you want to come and live with us.*
>
> *When you say your prayers, ask God to help reunite us.*
> *Will call you next week. God bless.*
> > *Love,*
> > *Dad and brother Bill*
>
> *P.S. We've taken some movies of our trip and we'll show them during your next visit.*

My own experience has been that most families exhibit, to varying degrees, the two patterns stated above. When the parents are at risk–that is, vulnerable to faulty perceptions related to their unresolved hurt and anger, they tend to project a great deal of the difficulty onto each other and, in a sense, encourage the children to be manipulative by taking sides. The reason for some couples being unable to cope with this situation is described in the form of an equation by Roman and Haddad: "Marriage failure plus grief, minus social approval multiplied by emotional distress and divided by low self-esteem, equals depression, anxiety, perhaps panic and the behavior these emotions elicit."[8]

One of the reactions I have observed regarding the child's experiences with divorce is that sometimes the older child, who is with the custodial parent, may take on the role of the absent parent. In a typical case where a young son is with his mother, for example, he may try to take on the father role and attempt to assume a great deal of responsibility. This responsibility is not only acted out in household chores, but also at the psychological level where the older child forms a strong alliance with the mother. On the other side we see children who feel sorry for the absent parent. They may begin to blame the custodial parent and take on the role of scapegoat in an attempt to bring the parents back together. The different responses of children are related to their ages, their birth order and, of course, the fact that each child is unique and each divorce brings with it a special situation for the child. If one were to generalize, one usually will find anger, fear and guilt manifesting themselves in the child's behavior. For the most part these manifestations are out of character and there may be frequent mood swings. It is important to note that most children have an ability to overcome crises and that with continued support of the child by the other parent, the child will bounce back from what is a normal state of confusion.

Now that we have had a chance to see the process which many families go through in a divorce, it is important to try to see the consequences of divorce as they relate specifically to children. Unhappily, one comes quickly to the conclusion that little scientific data is available which documents the effects of divorce on children. The studies reported are equivocal. There are both positive and negative effects of divorce on children for all ages. Cynthia Longfellow, in her extensive review of the research, feels that we are making a mistake when we ask the question, "Does divorce have negative effects?" Instead, our questions should be phrased to discover what it is about divorce that troubles children. In short, you cannot obtain the answers if you do not ask the right questions. She suggests a number of factors which may have to do with the child's adjustments: the life event changes that coincide with divorce, the single mother's emotional health, and the quality of the family's inter-relationships and outside support. Often overlooked is the fact that the degree to which any experience affects a child depends in part on the way it is assimilated and understood by the child.[9]

Most practitioners know that parents often do not tell the children much about the reasoning for their separation. Parents tend to be evasive and believe this will protect their children from being hurt. More damage is done by holding back an explanation for family breakdown because children usually feel guilty and blame themselves for the breakup. It is because of this guilt that children often attempt to take on the role of mediator and try to reconcile their parents. The child needs help to understand human frailties and difficulties and help to see their parents as less than perfect. It is ironic that when interviewing many couples they struggle with the questions as to when and how to tell the children. This inevitably is brought up at a significant time period following their decision to break up. In almost every case where I have interviewed the children subsequently, they have informed me that they were well aware that their parents were getting a divorce.

A number of studies point to the fact that one of the consequences of divorce is that many children develop low self-esteem. The children are described as being terribly worried that the remaining parent will also leave and that the child will feel that he is going to be orphaned. Some studies have mentioned the questioning attitude of children. If their parents who once loved each other no longer do, will they be the next to lose that love? The divorce introduces the idea that love can die. For the child who depends on the love of his or her parents, this can be a frightening thought. Other studies indicate the status consciousness of children. Such children may fear rejection and anticipate that friends and neighbors will make fun of them. They also know, from experience, that peers can be especially insensitive and make fun of them. It should be remembered that though these various responses are discussed separately they are not necessarily an either/or response. A child can experience all, or one, or none of them.[10]

When a child feels guilty, responsible, abandoned and rejected because of divorce there are emotional reactions. The child naturally develops a poor self-image, or low self-esteem. In a recent study conducted by Berg and Kelly, 177 children were interviewed. The children came from three different types of families. Group 1 came from families where the marriage was intact, but where the children felt "rejected," that is, they felt they had little communication with their parents. Group 2 came from families where the marriage was intact and the children felt accepted, that is, they felt they had good communication with their parents and a strong relationship. Group 3 came from divorced families where the children felt they had good communication with their parents. The results showed that the children of divorce did not differ in self-esteem from those children who came from intact-accepted families (Group 2). Children with the lowest self-esteem were those from Group 1. Many of these families had marital strife, or emotional divorce–an unsatisfactory, if stable marriage. The lessons here seem inescapable. Parents who have a good relationship with their children before divorce will probably continue to have a good relationship after divorce (though admittedly, strains may be put on that relationship). Children who viewed their families as undesirable had the lowest self-esteem even though their parents were still married. In short, the quality of the relationship between parents and their children is probably a more important factor in the child's psychological profile than whether or not his or her parents are still married.

This study and others indicate that the view of keeping the family together for the sake of the children is too simple and not necessarily in the best interests of the child.[11] From a review of the research there does appear to be a consensus that results support the notion that children are better off after a divorce than they are when they remain in a family situation with a high degree of conflict. In other words, following a divorce when the parents are in agreement for the most part, about child rearing and the child is involved with both parents, the result is better for this child than for the child remaining in the family where there is a great deal of arguing and unhappiness between the parents. This clearly points to the need for divorce mediation to help families adjust to the divorce in a way that will lead to families co-operating in resolving conflict rather than engaging in a pattern of destructive contention. The question of how the separation and divorce is handled as opposed to the breakdown itself is of great importance.

Often children who are in the midst of a bad marriage or a bad divorce will change their behavior in the classroom. Teachers will refer children who exhibit unusual withdrawal from play and school activities to a therapist. Such children may become sullen, find themselves unable to get along with other children and in general be overtaken by insecurity. It is not unusual for teachers to make referrals through the parents who are often so preoccupied with their own struggle that they are unaware of their children's difficulties.

A related example was noted in a conciliation court project: The nine year old boy who arrived with his mother and younger brother immediately announced that he was there "to get rid of his dad." However, half an hour later, when in the playroom and painting a giant black blob on the paper, he began to bitterly complain that his dad ignored him and always catered to his younger brother. He complained that his dad left his mother after only about 25 fights and he felt that he should have stayed until there had been at least 30 fights! He pointed out that his mother was very excitable and often upset and it was now up to him to try to settle her down after the continuing fights over access. "Getting rid of his dad" was obviously not the best solution for this child's complicated problems. In this case the conciliator discussed her impressions of the situation with both parents and lawyers. The lawyers, in understanding the situation, were able to see their clients' complaints regarding access in perspective and encourage co-operation "for the child's sake." The parents gained some insights about this boy's needs and began to deal with him and the question of visitation differently.[12]

Unhappily, the adversarial system may contribute to the attitude that the child or children are pawns–prizes who go to the winner. Parents, like it or not, are models for their children. Children of divorce react in a variety of ways, but often those ways reflect the actions of the parents. Like a mirror, the various emotional phases of the divorce may be seen in the actions of the children.

So great is their concern, the Family Court of Milwaukee, Wisconsin has seen fit to devise the following Bill of Rights of Children in divorce actions.[13]

I The right to be treated as an interested and affected person and not as a pawn, possession or chattel of either or both parents.

II The right to grow to maturity in that home environment which will best guarantee an opportunity for the child to grow to mature and responsible citizenship.

II The right to the day by day love, care, discipline and protection of the parent having custody of the child.

IV The right to know the non-custodial parent and to have the benefit of such parent's love and guidance through adequate visitations.

V The right to a positive and constructive relationship with both parents, with neither parent to be permitted to degrade or down-grade the other in the mind of the child.

VI The right to have moral and ethical values developed by precept and practices and have limits set for behavior so that the child early in life may develop self-discipline and self-control.

VII The right to the most adequate level of economic support that can be provided by the best efforts of both parents.

VII The right to the same opportunities for education that the child would have had if the family unit had not been broken.

IX The right to periodic review of custodial arrangements and child support orders as the circumstances of the parents and the benefit of the child may require.

X The right to recognition that children involved in a divorce are always disadvantaged parties and that the law must take affirmative steps to protect their welfare, including, where indicated, a social investigation to determine, and the appointment of a guardian *ad litem* to protect their interests.

Chapter Five

ESPECIALLY FOR YOUNG PEOPLE

"I remember that one of my first reactions was resentment. I knew both my parents were involved with other people and with their own careers. I knew they had grown far apart, but I wondered, How can they do this to me? In some ways, though, I was better off than my sister. She was more afraid than resentful."

This chapter is written for young people whose parents are contemplating separation, divorce, or whose families have already separated. Generally, it is intended for those over the age of thirteen, but if you have younger brothers and sisters you might read it and discuss with them some of the ideas presented.

Reading this material is not going to solve all your problems or end what you are going through. It is going to tell you what may occur, how you are going to be involved and where you can find someone with whom you can discuss your own personal problems. Every divorce case is different because the people involved are individuals, because the laws vary from place to place and because, while similarities exist, no two situations are exactly alike.

Let's start with some honesty. You love both your parents and you really want them to stay together. The chances are, however, that you can't help them get back together. You *can* help make things easier for them and for yourself.

This year, over one million people will get divorced. Many more will become separated or try what is called a "trial separation." This may be terribly difficult for their children because children often feel that they must choose between their parents.

It is a time of confusion and mixed emotions. Many questions arise–unfortunately, they are questions which are extremely difficult to answer. One common question is–how can two people fall out of love? And, who is to blame for divorce?

As you know, the love that two adults feel for one another is quite different than the love they feel for their children. People who live together usually experience periods of tension. Sometimes they resolve their difficulties, sometimes the tensions grow worse and the couple decides to part company. People who fall out of love with one another go on loving their children. It is important for you to realize this.

Let's have a closer look at some of the questions you may be asking.

Who's to blame for divorce? Now, let's think about why this question is being asked in the first place. Does it matter? This is the question you may want to ask because you may think it will help you make some kind of choice, if indeed you have to make a choice. It is also the question the legal system may ask. Our legal system as it is presently set up is, unhappily, designed to "find fault"–to find out who is to blame. But, legal definitions of "fault" do not often apply to human relationships. When people are involved in getting a separation and divorce they are often angry at one another. They blame each other and say and do things that they would not do under normal circumstances. When you ask, "Who's to blame?" you may really be saying, "Am I to blame?" or, "Which parent should I choose?"

It is not necessary for you to "choose" which parent you love the most. You probably love them both. As for the unspoken question, "Am I to blame?" the answer is *no*. The answer is *no* even if you are sometimes the focus of your parents' arguments. People who are deeply angry with one another may fight over the way coffee is prepared or how one of them is treating you. Not all people who are angry fight, of course. Some of them simply cease speaking to one another and fill rooms with sullen silence. In either case, you must realize that you are not the cause of the problem. In other words, it is not so important to know who *is* to blame as it is for you to realize *you are not to blame.*

Your younger brothers and sisters might be afraid. They may wonder if your mother and father, who have fallen out of love with one another, could fall out of love with them. You can help reassure them that this won't happen.

The next important question is, "What can I do?" Earlier, it was indicated that you probably couldn't help solve your parents' problems. If you plead for them to stay together you may only make them feel more guilty. Guilt is not a healthy basis for family life. Look around you! You probably have many friends whose parents don't get along well, but who still live together. The chances are that their family life is disturbing and that they complain they can't communicate with their parents.

Having parents who are separated or divorced is probably not as bad as it sounds, especially if you can maintain a good relationship with them. There are a few simple things you can do to ensure a good future relationship. First, do not take sides. Talk to your parents together and tell them you love them both and you are not giving up your relationship with either of them. One or both of your parents may try to "win" you over to their side. They may try to talk about the other parent to you. People in a highly emotional state do this because they need support, but it can be damaging. Try always to talk to your parents together and not allow yourself to be drawn into a situation where you may be siding with one or the other.

If your parent will not listen, it is important that you seek out help for yourself. Frankly, even if your parents are not arguing or bitter, divorce is upsetting. You should find someone to talk to, someone who is not involved. It is wise not to choose a relative. An aunt, uncle or grandparents are not necessarily impartial. You can begin with your school counselor. He or she can refer you to someone specific. Many Family Service Associations offer counseling to young people and in many communities and some schools there are special youth clinics. Some schools and community associations also have seminars for young people whose parents are getting a separation or divorce. In these seminars you will find other young people who have the same kinds of problems you have.

In some places it is now possible for young people whose parents are divorcing to have their own lawyer. This is something you should discuss with a counselor–again, if you don't know where to start, start at school.

The next question is, "What will happen when my parents get divorced?" The answer to this question depends on your parents' attitude, on whether or not they have opted for divorce mediation, the main subject of this book, on the legal system where you live, and on the community services available.

If your parents agree to try divorce mediation first, the mediator will also talk to you. He or she will likely talk to you alone and with your parents. You will be able to express your feelings openly because the mediator is not "on the side" of either of your parents.

Perhaps you will live with one parent all the time, perhaps you will live with one parent and then the other, or perhaps you will visit one parent and live with the other. Discuss your feelings openly with both your parents. Whatever the arrangement, you should be determined to keep your relationship with both your parents as natural and as close as possible. They may not want to see one another, but they will want to see and be with you. As time passes it *will* get easier. Most young people fear the change more than they react to the reality, which when it comes, is often a relief. The young person whose story follows has been through it . . . perhaps her feelings and experiences are similar to your own. Her comments are unedited and appear just as she wrote them down for me. Her parents have been separated for two years.

"Today, I'm seventeen years old and live with my mother and younger sister. My parents both began to argue with each other about two years before they separated. Then, I was twelve and my sister was eight. I remember one night as being particularly terrible. I remember it because that was the night separation was first mentioned for real. My sister and I were downstairs in the family room building tents out of sleeping bags. Then my sister and I heard Mom and Dad upstairs. My sister went upstairs to listen. She came back crying and said that Mommy was leaving. We both started to cry and we were both scared. When our parents found out we had heard everything they both cried too. Mommy said she wasn't leaving us and promised she wouldn't go anywhere without us. We were both really upset because we were afraid we would wake up one morning and find one of our parents gone. The thought of moving was also scary. We liked the house, our schools and our friends. Since things were such a mess at home, the familiar circumstances and staying in one place became really important to both of us.

"I remember that one of my first reactions was resentment. I knew both my parents were involved with other people and with their own careers. I knew they had grown far apart, but I wondered, How can they do this to me? In some ways, though, I was better off than my sister. She was more afraid than resentful.

"My parents started going to a marriage counselor. They didn't fight as much, but they didn't talk to each other much either. Then I went to the marriage counselor too. I don't think she helped me much because she didn't understand me. She asked who I wanted to live with and took notes.

"Finally, after a long time, my dad decided to move out of the house. I remember that I wasn't worried about my life without my dad as much as I was worried about what the neighbors would think and say. I also remember feeling guilty. As though there was something I should have done, but didn't.

"My father moved into an apartment a few blocks away. As soon as he was gone, he and Mother began to get on much better. He moved out in November and that first Christmas he was gone was really strange, mostly because things seemed so different.

"Gradually, things really improved. It is understood that my sister and I can go to my father's whenever we want and that my dad can come here whenever he wants. We don't go there often because there isn't anything to do, but he comes here at least once a week for dinner or sometimes twice a week. Sometimes he takes us all out and sometimes he takes only my sister and me out. In the summer we go on holiday with my dad (sometimes to Europe to visit my grandparents) for two or three weeks or a month. When my mother goes on vacation Dad comes and lives in the house with us. If we are going someplace with our own friends and my dad is here, we just go ahead and leave. That way our relationship with our dad is natural. My sister is the same and not scared anymore.

"Sometimes I miss my dad because he is not around all the time, but I don't miss the hostility that so often made me cry. I have thought about it a lot and I realize that my parents are very different people. They have really worked hard at trying to get along so we wouldn't be hurt anymore and both of them try to talk to us and to listen. In some ways my sister and I have the best of both worlds. I have friends whose parents are still married, but who don't get along with their parents. I also have friends whose parents are divorced and don't speak to each other. My sister and I went through a bad period, but now our parents talk to each other like friends and we have a good relationship with both of them. It's more important to have a good relationship with your parents than it is to have your parents living in one house together. We feel very lucky because our parents get on better now and their separation has not turned out to be as bad as we imagined such a thing would be."

Not all young people feel as this girl does, but time does help. The Association of Family Conciliation Courts publishes a pamphlet called *Parents are Forever*. It is essentially a guideline for parents, but it is reproduced here because it says some things you, as a young person, should be aware of. You might want to sit down with your parents and go over some of these points with them. Openly discuss visiting with them, don't take sides, and, if necessary, find someone you can talk to. Ask your school counselor, check the phone book under Family Conciliation Courts or Family Service Association, consult a clergyman, or phone your local mental health association. Any one of these persons or organizations can recommend a place in your community where you can find help. Even if you feel that you don't need help you will feel better just by talking things over with an experienced, impartial person who will keep your confidence.

Dear Parent,

As you know, a divorce or separation decree cannot and does not end your responsibility as a parent. PARENTS ARE FOREVER. Both parents should make every attempt to continue to play a vital part in the lives of their children. Children need the ongoing interest and concern of their parents. Children must feel they have two parents who love them, even though those parents could not live happily with each other.

It is our hope that the information in this pamphlet will assist you in helping your children cope with your divorce or separation with a minimum of hurt. The practical guidelines which follow are based on the many years of experience of court marriage and family counselors.

If you are like most people, you probably have some feelings of isolation, despair, depression, loneliness, grief, guilt and a loss of self-confidence. You are worried about many things, such as finances, a new social life, employment, fulfillment of sexual needs and the welfare of your children. You can use this present time of difficulty as an opportunity for growth or a surrender to self-pity.

The way you feel about yourself will affect the way your children feel about themselves. **The way you cope with your divorce will in large part determine how your children cope with it.** Yes, you are at a cross-roads and can choose from alternative routes.

One road leads to self-pity, living the past, nurturing bitterness and turning the children against your former marriage partner. This is a dead-end road which spells trouble for you and your children.

The other road, and the constructive one, leads to becoming involved with experiences that provide opportunities for you to again feel success, to get to know yourself better, restore your self-confidence, reach out for goals that will make your life productive, satisfying and meaningful.

The task of all parents, whether or not a marriage continues, is not easy. All parents make mistakes. But if you have a good relationship with your children and they feel your love and acceptance, they will soon forget your mistakes and remember only your goodness.

Guidelines for Parents

As we have already indicated, the way you cope with your divorce will in large part determine how your children cope with it. Try to use the experience of divorce as an opportunity for personal growth, not defeat. In this way you can continue to be effective as a parent and to not only effectively meet your children's needs, but just as important, your own needs as a person. Continuing conflict between you and your marriage partner during and after divorce can interfere with your effectiveness as a parent.

1. **Allow yourself and your children time for readjustment**. Convalescence from an emotional operation such as divorce or separation is essential.

2. **Remember the best parts of your marriage.** Share them with your children and use them constructively whether or not you have custody.

3. **Assure your children that they are not to blame for the breakup and that they are not being rejected or abandoned**. Children, especially the young ones, often feel they have done something wrong and believe the problems in the family are the results of their misdeeds. Small children may feel that some action or secret wish of theirs has caused the trouble between their parents.

4. **Continuing anger or bitterness toward your former partner can injure your children far more than the divorce or separation itself. The feelings you show are more important than the words you use.**

5. **Refrain from voicing criticism of the other parent.** It is

difficult but absolutely necessary for a child's healthy development. It is important that the child respect both parents.

6. **Do not force or encourage your children to take sides.** To do so encourages frustration, guilt and resentment.

7. **Try not to upset a child's routine too abruptly.** Children need a sense of continuity and it is disturbing to them if they must cope with too many changes at once.

8. **Divorce or separation often leads to financial pressures on both parents.** When there is a financial crisis, the parents' first impulse may be to try to keep the children from realizing it. Often, they would rather make sacrifices themselves than ask the child to do so. The atmosphere is healthier when there is frankness and when children are expected to help.

9. **Marriage breakdown is always hard on the children.** They may not always show their distress or realize at first what this will mean to them. Parents should be direct and simple in telling children what is happening and why, and in a way a child can understand and digest. This will vary with the circumstances and each child's age and comprehension. The worst course is to try and hush things up and make children feel they must not talk or even think about what they sense is going on. Unpleasant happenings need explanation which should be brief, prompt, direct and honest.

10. **The story of your divorce or separation may have to be retold after the children get older and consider life more maturely.** Though it would be unfortunate to present either situation as a tragedy and either parent as a martyr, it would be a pity also to pretend there are no regrets and that the breakdown of a marriage is so common it hardly matters.

11. **The guilt parents may feel about the marriage breakdown may interfere in their disciplining the children.** A child needs consistent control and direction. Over-permissiveness, or indecisive parents who leave a child at the

mercy of every passing whim and impulse interfere with a child's healthy development. Children need and want to know quite clearly what is expected of them. Children feel more secure when limits are set. They are confused when grown-ups seem to permit behavior which they themselves know to be wrong and are trying to outgrow. Children need leadership and sometimes authority. Parents must be ready to say "NO" when necessary.

Visitation Guidelines

The behavior of parents has a great influence on the emotional adjustment of their children. This is equally true after the breakdown of a marriage. The following visitation guidelines have been found to be helpful in achieving meaningful visits:

1. It is important to try to maintain contact between the child and the parent who has left home. Maintaining some form of contact helps the child deal with his fantasies which are much worse than the reality of what is happening; helps to decrease feelings of rejection; decreases feelings that the divorce happened because he is a bad child; reduce his feelings that he may never see the other parent again.

2. Visits should be pleasant not only for the children but for both parents. Visitation should help your children maintain a positive relationship with their visiting parent. It is important that neither parent verbally or physically attack the other parent in the presence of the children. Children tend to view such attacks as attacks on them.

3. The parent with whom the children live must prepare them physically and emotionally for the visit. The children should be available promptly at the time mutually agreed upon and returned at the time agreed upon.

4. The visits should not take place only in the children's home. The visiting parent may wish the children to visit in his or her home overnight, or may want to plan an enjoyable outing.

5. The question is often asked, "Should the father take the children to the girlfriend's house?" The same question is asked about the mother if she is the non-custodial parent. Visitation is the time for the children and parent to be with each other; to enjoy each other; to maintain positive relationships. Having other people participate may dilute the parent-child experience during visitation. However, it should not be ruled out altogether. Avoid "parades."

6. Visits should be as frequent as practical. Any schedules established should be flexible. Should scheduled visits need to be cancelled (and sometimes they have to be), inform the other parent as soon as possible with a full and honest explanation to the child.

7. You may need to adjust the visitation schedule from time to time according to your children's age, health and interests.

8. Frequently non-custodial parents ask why they should visit. They are hurt; feel they are no longer needed; the custodial parent has the home and the children. The visit is one of the few times that the non-custodial parent has personal contact with the children and for that reason it should be a meaningful one for both the non-custodial parent and the children. Even though the parents have not been able to get along, the children still need both parents.

9. Often, the non-custodial parent questions where they should take the children on the visits and what they should plan in the way of amusement for them, particularly if the children are young. Activities may add to the pleasure of the visit, but most important of all is the non-custodial parent's involvement with the children. A giving of self is more important than whatever material things they may get.

10. The visit should not be used to check on the other parent. Children should not be pumped for this kind of information. They should not be used as little spies. Often in the children's perception the parents hate each other and the children will feel uncomfortable at the time of the

visits. In the children's mind, if they do anything to please the visiting parent, they may invite outright rejection by their other parent. They may feel they have already lost one parent and are fearful of losing the other. For these reasons, parents should show mutual respect for each other.

11. The children may be left with many problems following visits and both parents should make every effort to discuss them and to agree on ways to deal with them.

12. Both parents should strive for agreement in decisions pertaining to the children, especially discipline, so that one parent is not undermining the other parent's efforts.

If You Need Help

It is unfortunate that many people believe that to ask for help is a sign of weakness, for in reality it is a sign of strength. It takes a great deal of courage for a person to say "I have a problem which I cannot solve alone and I need help with it."

Asking for help does not mean people are incapable of solving their problems. For in the final analysis, it is the people themselves who solve their problems. Counselors merely guide people and give some direction to their search for solutions. There are a few people who have not needed help at some time in their lives. Those who reach for professional help in times of crisis have a better chance of finding effective and permanent solutions in a shorter time.

Persons with problems often become discouraged which only emphasizes weaknesses. They often overlook strengths still present as well as other alternatives for coping with these problems. A trained counselor may assist in achieving a better understanding of strengths or weaknesses.

Advice from well-meaning friends and relatives, in many cases, may further aggravate the situation. Friends or relatives usually are not professionally trained to treat problems and they can seldom be objective.

Professional counseling may create an awareness which can assist you in dealing with your and your children's problems at this time.

Chapter Six

A MULTI-FACETED SYSTEM

The mediator does give advice on certain issues, spelling out the advantages and disadvantages, but being very careful not to take sides with individual family members. He will suggest some new options regarding some problems so that family members may make a more realistic decision. What this means is that the resolution of the dispute is based on the interpersonal process between and among family members. The decisions made are those of the family. It is for this reason that a communications approach is fundamental to the divorce mediation method of solving family disputes.

Marriage counseling often deals with an intensive long-term approach. Its primary goal is to help people become more effective within their marriage; in other words, marriage counseling is designed to enhance the marital relationship through various techniques that will improve communication between the partners. There is a tendency to lump all forms of therapy that deal with marriage or the issues of marriage and divorce under the heading "marriage counseling." Divorce mediation, however, is *not* marriage counseling. It is a method of resolving divorce issues by adapting mediation and arbitration approaches. It is a method of constructively resolving disputes.

Divorce mediation is a process of rational mediation between conflicting spouses.[1] The mediator acts as a neutral third party, one who has the freely-given power to assist in resolution. The interests of the children are paramount to the mediator. In all cases, the role of the mediator is to direct discussion into pro-ductive channels, to encourage compromise, to take the attitude of problem solving and to prevent the type of name-calling and tawdry recrimination so prevalent in the courtroom.

The most important goals of divorce mediation are to help the family arrive at an amicable settlement, to ensure that the children's interests come first and to help parents and children understand that divorced couples are still mothers and fathers. Even if a couple has privately resolved all relevant issues related to their children, there is still good reason to enter into a mediation procedure. The mediator has an independent goal apart from the narrowly defined interests of the spouses, in that his or her over-riding responsibility is to ensure the welfare of the children.

The welfare of the children remains the central focus of all discussion and/or agreements, no matter what the specific topic. The mediator's role is *advisory*, but he or she also serves as a catalyst who encourages spouses to identify areas of disagreement directly related to separation and the settlement of their own disputes. The basis of mediation is personal responsibility and interpersonal recognition, if not respect.

Normally the points covered in mediation and arbitration will be custody, visitation rights and maintenance. Sometimes the participants will determine the subjects to be discussed in advance, but these advance topics may be expanded or contracted during the process.

Let us examine first some of the skills involved in such an interview and then the mechanics of how this method actually works.

Interviewing Skills

When working with families, the mediator considers communication as the *sine-qua-non* of family operations. All communication, verbal or non-verbal, in some ways describes the nature of the relationship between and among the members of the family. Accordingly, all behavior has interactional significance and can be thought of as synonymous with communication. This became apparent from what has become a well-known principle, that "one cannot *not* communicate." The husband who comes home from work and says nothing to his wife and children as he walks past them in the family room is really communicating something. The mediator is constantly helping family members clarify indirect and distorted messages. He does this primarily by engaging the family members themselves in talking to each other. He will be observing how the family or couple interact so that he or she can understand how the family operates. The mediator will also pay close attention to ways messages are sent and received as well as the degree of clarity, and directness of communication. He will try to reduce the destructive conflict and set a framework for non-accusatory blaming from one member to the other. He will try to clarify faulty communication by giving the family members an opportunity to make some of the implicit communication explicit.

It is only through understanding that the couple or family can move into dispute resolution. The mediator engages the family members by asking direct questions and framing the questions so that members in the interview relate to each other and to the mediator. An example might be, "Would you tell your husband what you feel right now," or, "You seem puzzled at what she just said, so why don't you ask her to explain more clearly what she means?"

The mediator does give advice on certain issues, spelling out the advantages and disadvantages, but being very careful not to take sides with individual family members. He will suggest some new options regarding some problems so that family members may make a more realistic decision. What this means is that the resolution of the dispute is based on the interpersonal process between and among family members. The decisions made are those of the family. It is for this reason that a communications approach is fundamental to the divorce mediation method of solving family disputes.

The Procedures of the Method

The Initial Phase: Exploration

   The first discussions are usually carried out with each individual family member. It is critical for the mediator to thoroughly explain the mediation process at this time. This is a period of individual introspection and the mediator simply tries to understand where each individual stands as well as what each wants to accomplish. The mediator will listen to what is said, but will also observe what is done.
   The mediator's ability to empathize is critical to this phase. He or she must be able to accept, understand and support the family member so that real expression can take place.
   The focus is not only on how the individual feels about a specific problem at hand, but also on self-perception. This process creates an atmosphere of trust between client and mediator. The major intent is to identify and clarify problems, while offering constant emotional support. Each relevant family member is approached in the same way: given an opportunity to ventilate the anger and hurt according to each person's unique situation while being able to explore and focus on his or her unique problems.

Second Phase: Problem Solving

   This is the critical negotiation phase which eventually leads to the resolution of disputes. During this period it is extremely important that family members interact with each other. The focus during this phase shifts from the mediator to the family, when joint interviews are held with the couple, or with the entire family if the situation demands collective consultation. Each person explains his or her goals and expresses what is *really* wanted.
   The individual positions which were discovered in phase one are discussed among the parties involved. These views are

discussed in two ways: (1) as stated by the individual and (2) as they are *understood* by other family members.

This latter point is extremely important and warrants further explanation. The American humorist, Oliver Wendell Holmes, once wrote a short piece entitled *The Three Johns* as part of his larger work, *The Autocrat at the Breakfast Table*. Its theme was that "John" was not one person, but three persons. He was (1) John as he perceived himself; (2) John as perceived by his conversational partner; and (3) John as he actually is. The idea was simple–for every two people in a conversation there are, in reality six. Tongue in cheek, Holmes goes on to illustrate the real difficulties of communication between two individuals who are in reality six. As the old saying goes, "Never mind what I say, listen to what I mean." This is, more often than not, the task of the mediator. A wife might say to her estranged husband, "You can see the children whenever you want. Just call before you come." The wife is asking her estranged mate to respect her privacy, but what exactly does "call before you come" mean? The husband might well interpret this to mean he should call twenty minutes before arriving when, in fact, the wife meant she wanted two days' warning. This is an oversimplified example of misunderstanding in communication, but it illustrates the role of the mediator. He or she must be certain that people express their real desires and goals and, equally important, that the other party understands. By clearing up family communication, the mediator assists in clarifying ambiguous issues. The mediator helps the family members go beyond the initial presenting problem so that they may have a firmer grasp of the *real* problems.

When there is an impasse, the mediator attempts to reframe the conflict by broadening perspectives and offering options not previously realized. For example, in a situation where the parents are in disagreement as to the amount of time children should spend with each of them, they may be so concerned with their own objectives that they have not considered what would be best for their children. The mediator can help the parents see how they must set aside their own personal interests when those interests conflict with the best interests of the children. This is usually brought about during discussions with the children and parents together.

Final Phase: Resolution

This phase of divorce mediation usually takes a highly-structured form. It is nearly contractual in nature and details what each party will do.

Each step is monitored so that everyone concerned knows what action is being taken on any agreements made. If anyone does not act as agreed there will be almost immediate feedback. This reduces the "revolving door syndrome" of going back to the courts.

In many cases the emotional entanglement during separation, and later, may lead to a great deal of resentment on the part of one individual in the family. Before proper mediation can be effective, this individual may need to take advantage of more intensive psychological therapy outside the mediation process. This type of therapy is called *crisis intervention* and is also short-term. It may be simultaneous with the divorce mediation process.

It is important to understand that the mediator will be taking a "systems" approach to the family. That is, if one member is affected, the entire family "system" is also affected. It is therefore crucial that the mediator be able to see all family members who may be involved. The best way to describe the role of the mediator would be to define him or her as a "facilitator." The mediator's main objective is the resolution of family disputes in the context of what is best for the children.

The divorce mediation system is at least in part a combination of traditional labor relations techniques and the ability to understand the nuances of interpersonal relationships. The problem remains, of course, of how to implement this combined knowledge when dealing with divorce, a problem that seems on the surface to be unlike either a labor dispute or an administrative tribunal.

To sum up, the mediator must: provide emotional support, help identify the problem or problems, elicit sufficient factual information to find a solution to the problem, develop and identify all possible alternative solutions, evaluate the probable outcome of alternative solutions, assist the couple to mutually select one of the alternatives and develop an agreement as to the steps which must be taken in order for the selected alternative to be successful, and follow up or monitor the success of such an agreement.

Marriage is not, after all, a corporate merger. It is a willing participation in a social and emotional contract. The advantage of divorce mediation is that divorce is not viewed as any one individual's fault, but rather as a common responsibility. It is not for the courts to solve our interpersonal problems nor can we abdicate our own responsibilities for the conduct of our lives and those of our children.

It is neither desirable nor necessary for individual lawyers to be taking any legal action during the divorce mediation process. The absence of lawyers at this point, quite apart from the expense involved, helps prevent the old specters of the adversary system (fault finding and blame) from getting in the way of the issues at hand. *In order to protect both spouses and the mediator, all meetings, information presented, or offers made are considered confidential and are not available for any subsequent court proceedings. In this way, the mediator will not degenerate into yet another "expert" witness.* To make sure, the mediator will require as a precondition that he or she will not be called later to testify or produce documents in a courtroom. This is important to the spouses because it helps them feel at ease. They know they can discuss their feelings with a degree of openness and candor that will make it easier to arrive at a resolution.

Some lawyers also become uneasy when confronted with the divorce mediation process. They instruct their clients not to reveal certain information for fear that it will be held against them in a subsequent court case. In an instance where lawyers have already been engaged, it is of the utmost importance that they be cognizant of the mediation process and that they be reassured that information discussed is considered privileged. To ensure the highest degree of co-operation I always have the lawyers and my clients sign an agreement which includes a clause stating that "Evidence of anything said or of any admission or communication made in the course of mediation is not admissible in the pending or any other legal proceedings. The mediator may not be called as a witness or on behalf of either parent (party) in the pending or any other legal proceeding, and the mediator shall not be required or permitted in the pending or any other legal proceeding to give opinion or to disclose any admission or communication made to him in the course of mediation." We will examine this agreement further on and elaborate on the role of the mediator.

Due to the undeniable legal implication of divorce, the mediator should meet privately with individual lawyers, accountants, or any other relevant persons where such meetings might be appropriate. Each spouse is encouraged to fully disclose all information (financial statements, tax returns, and the like) that are requested either by the mediator or the other spouse when such information has an important bearing on the discussion. This type of discussion falls into the "fact finding" phase of the divorce mediation process.

Divorce mediation is not intended to be extended family therapy. There are agencies as well as private practitioners that provide family and marriage counseling, and such groups and individuals do provide long term therapy. The length of divorce mediation meetings as well as their number and frequency can be determined once it is clear that the entire process will be beneficial to the whole family. In any event, the number of meetings is not extended to the point where they might unduly delay legal divorce proceedings or increase costs. As a hedge against the mediation meetings becoming protracted, the couple may jointly specify an outward limit–six to ten meetings, for example. Fluidity is of prime importance, so all such limits may be waived at any time with the consent of all concerned.

Though maximum limits may be fluid, minimum limits should be firmly set. If mediation is entered into voluntarily, then a minimum limit of perhaps two meetings should be required. If, however, mediation or conciliation are ordered by the court, there is usually a limit of two meetings with a maximum of six. The Los Angeles Conciliation Court, for instance, requires one session of approximately one and one-half hours. During this meeting, the spouses are usually seen together first for a brief period to enable the conciliator to establish the ground rules, satisfy them of his or her impartiality, and to assure them that the welfare of the children is of primary importance. The parents are then seen separately and the entire session ends with a tripartite conference. If it appears that the process will be beneficial, a second meeting might be scheduled. From that point other meetings can be arranged if progress is being made and if the process is improving the situation.

Once the couple is satisfied that mediation really is a rational and helpful alternative to the courts, that the mediator is impartial, and that the interests of the children come first, then attempts at a divorce settlement can begin. If agreement is reached, the details are written down, signed by the spouses and shown to the respective lawyers. This agreement is then submitted to the court as the basis of the divorce decree. The agreement comes solely from the mediation process and has nothing to do with fault or the adversary system. It is a result of mutual co-operative problem solving.

Let us examine one of my cases as an example of how the divorce mediation process works.

Mr. Clark is a machinist who makes a fair income working in a large industrial plant. Mrs. Clark is a housewife who has spent most of her time in the home. They have been together for eleven years and have one child, Grace. Before I came into contact with them they had already decided to separate. They had been to a marriage counselor and both had realized that they were basically unsuited to each other. They also recognized they had been in a long-term destructive relationship and that effective communication was no longer possible. The Clarks were referred to me by their respective lawyers. The immediate problem was custody and visitation rights with regard to their daughter. Part of their decision to enter into mediation had to do with their lawyers' realization that the traditional adversary system was simply not working–for all the reasons we have previously discussed–and that the Clarks' relationship was deteriorating. During the adversarial process, for example, there had been numerous occasions when the child had been dragged in and been made a victim of the battle between the parents. The lawyers themselves were at a stand-off, and in fact, were having great difficulty communicating between themselves.

Since I was seeing the Clarks at the lawyers' request, the terms of mediation were clearly set out in the lawyers' referral.[2] The form reproduced below, received from the Clarks' lawyers, is a joint referral, but single referrals are often presented. Any number of alterations may be made to this basic format. Each referral is tailored to individual client needs.

Dear _____ ,

Mr. and Mrs. Clark, by their Counsel, hereby refer to you for mediation questions relating to custody of their child.

It is understood that you consent to act as mediator and this letter will set out the terms upon which the mediation is to proceed. They are:

1) As mediator, you will attempt to bring about an agreement between the father and the mother as to the determination of the following questions:

   a) How much time should the child spend with each parent during school summer vacation?

   b) Should custody of the child be changed from the mother to the father?

2) In considering these questions, the parents and the mediator shall give primary importance to the needs of the child and how these needs, in the circumstances, can best be met.

3) In working out the custody and access arrangement which best meets the needs of the child, the parents may agree that:

a) One or other of them shall have temporary custody of the child for a trial period; or

b) Both of them shall have custody of the child as joint custodians, or first one parent then the other, during periods that are specified and set out in the agreement; or

c) neither of the parents shall have custody of the child but the periods of time which each child is to be with each parent are to be specified and set out in the agreement.

These alternatives are mentioned for the purpose of emphasizing that the parties are to make whatever arrangement is in the best interests of the child. Their choice may be one of these alternatives, or any better alternative that might emerge from the mediation meetings.

4) The separation agreement entered into under date of the _____ day of _____ , 19 _____ , shall not be binding on the parties so far as the questions of custody and access are concerned.

5) The question of the child's maintenance or financial support is excluded from mediation and, if it arises, shall be referred back to Counsel for determination.

6) In attempting to bring about an agreement, the mediator may meet with and speak to the father, the mother, and the child separately, or jointly, and may consult such other persons and inspect such reports, records, or documents as he deems necessary.

7) Any agreement reached shall constitute a settlement of the subjects under mediation and be produced for the information of the court in the legal proceedings pending between the father and the mother in the Supreme Court of _____ or in any other relevant proceedings.

8) In the event that no agreement is reached within the period established for mediation, both parties shall have the right to pursue their legal remedies in the action pending between them in the Supreme Court of _____ or in such other action or proceedings as they or either of them may be advised to take.

9) The period of time allowed for the mediation shall be established by the mediator in consultation with both Counsel after the mediator has interviewed both parents, but in no event shall be for more than six weeks from the date of this letter.

10) Evidence of anything said or of any admission or communication made in the course of mediation is not admissible in the pending or any other legal proceeding.

11) The mediator will not be called as a witness or on behalf of either parent in the pending or any other legal proceeding, and the mediator shall not be required or permitted in the pending or any other legal proceeding to give any opinion or to disclose any admission or communication made to him in the course of mediation.

12) Except to inform Counsel that:
   a) No agreement has been reached; or
   b) What the terms of the agreement are,
   there shall be no report made by the mediator of the mediation process.

13) Your fee for mediation shall be borne by the parents in equal shares and payable on such terms as are determined by you.

Mediation is agreed to by both parents in the confident expectation that, with your assistance, they can determine the questions above, in a way that will be more satisfactory than any settlement imposed by a court or other process.

Please feel free to telephone either Counsel at any time for whatever information or assistance that they might be in a position to give. Counsel will refrain from initiating any contact with you in order to give you full freedom to act without interference.

We thank you for consenting to this referral and for acting as mediator.

Yours very truly,

Once the basic ground rules were set, divorce mediation was further defined to the couple. Any agreement reached would constitute a settlement of the subjects under dispute. Only this agreement, unlike an arbitrator's report, would be given to the court in the legal proceedings pending between them. If no agreement was reached in mediation the parents were free to pursue their dispute through the adversarial system. The period of time allowed for dispute resolution using divorce mediation would be established once Mr. and Mrs. Clark had been interviewed and after consultation with their lawyers, but for no reason would it be extended beyond the six-week time limit.

Point 10 of the referral letter was reiterated to assure the couple that none of the information gathered would be admissible in any legal proceeding. The mediator would only inform counsel either that no agreement had been obtained or, if an agreement was reached, what its terms were.

The final stipulation was that the mediator's fee would be borne equally by Mr. and Mrs. Clark. Neither spouse was constrained by the rule-bound procedures of adversarial divorce. Some rules are usually necessary, but the more rules that are imposed, the fewer choices the spouses have and the fewer opportunities there are for compromise. One of the key features of divorce mediation is that the parties have the opportunity to choose the mediator. This obviously goes a long way in establishing the necessary trust between the couple and the mediator.

The next step in this case was to discuss mediation with the two lawyers involved. They were encouraged to share their perceptions of their clients' positions. In turn, I clarified my role reiterating my position as the child's advocate. In the Clarks' case, mediation could prevent a lengthy and bitter court battle which neither party could afford either financially or psychologically.

Following discussions with the lawyers, Mr. and Mrs. Clark were interviewed separately. Then Grace was seen alone. My impression was that the parents as well as the child were suffering from battle fatigue, as there had been a long, hard series of conflicts with nothing but a hollow victory looming in the far distance. The parents were visibly relieved that I was not interested in determining who was the most suitable parent, but rather in creating a climate for equitable negotiation.

The most important and encouraging result of mediation in this case was that for the first time the couple worked *together* to arrive at a suitable living arrangement for their daughter. They made a decision for her without giving their eleven-year-old the kind of Hobson's choice that had previously produced nothing but guilt and conflict. They decided on a system of shared parenting. This system is a vital offshoot of divorce mediation and is discussed in a separate chapter. A typical letter of agreement as the result of mediation is produced below:

Dear Judge _____ :
    Through a voluntary process of Divorce Mediation, Mr. and Mrs. _____ have arrived at a negotiated settlement regarding the custody of their child.
    Mrs. _____ agrees that Mr. _____ will have access to the child on alternate weekends. All holidays will be split equally between the parents. Mr. _____ agrees that Mrs. _____ will have legal custody of the children.
    Both parties agree that these arrangements will continue until such time as there is a substantial change. At such time, the terms of this agreement will be renegotiated with the aid of a mediator.
                    Yours sincerely,

            Mr. _____

            Mrs. _____

For Grace this was a positive solution which she gladly accepted. Mr. and Mrs. Clark knew that their marriage was over and, not surprisingly, Grace also acknowledged this fact in her own words. Still, she did not want to lose either of them, nor did she want to become a pawn for some courtroom game. Although children often cannot express their feelings in easily understood terms, they are usually quite aware of what is happening to their parents and to them.

The Clarks' use of divorce mediation was not total. They did go on to use the adversary system to settle other matters in their divorce. Nevertheless, progress was made, relief felt and the reasonable attitudes established did make it possible for them to arrive at an equitable divorce.

Like the Morrows, the Clarks were not actually angry with anyone. Under normal and proper circumstances they were willing to negotiate with each other.

There are, of course, people who are unable to settle a dispute by mediation. Some are furious with the former spouse and are seeking revenge. This may be related to an unresolved emotional attachment that one spouse still has for the other and, combined with getting into the process of the adversarial system where accusations and counter-accusations are hurled at one another, bitterness and the desire for revenge are increased. Once this happens, a kind of psychological warfare exists and often mediation cannot reverse the situation or penetrate the attitudes of the adversaries. Some people must have their "day in court" regardless of the circumstances. In these unhappy cases the mediator simply must report that the combatants have been unable to reach an agreement. He or she must quietly withdraw from the scene and remove all the privileged information acquired.

Where negotiation is impossible, there are three options available (see Figure 1):

1) The spouses may choose to go to the courts and use the adversary system as a vehicle for their resentment and all proceedings commence *de novo* (anew);
2) They may choose binding arbitration; or
3) they may choose advisory arbitration.

In *binding* arbitration the spouses agree in advance that the decision of the arbitrator will be binding on them with the same force as a court order.

In *advisory* arbitration they are free to accept or reject the substance of the arbitrator's award. If they accept, the decision will be considered binding, but if they opt for rejection, they may then apply to the courts for final determination. If the courts are used, however, it will be made clear to the couple, in advance, that the arbitrator's report will be made available to the judge. One of the difficulties with this latter method is that it once again removes the decision-making responsibility from the parents. In effect, the judge is replaced in the traditional adversarial approach with an arbitrator. However, the arbitra-

Figure 1

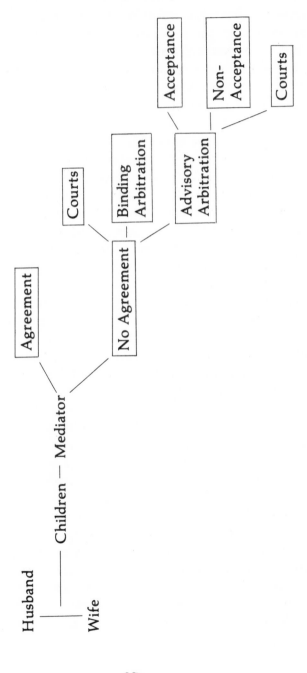

tor, unlike the judge, has the advantage of interviewing all the relevant parties, gathering information from the various sources and drawing upon his interviewing skills and knowledge of human behavior. One could describe the approach as less than ideal, but, in certain circumstances, preferable to a court trial.

When the above method is used it has to be explained to the spouses that the information gathered is not confidential nor privileged and that it will be made available in any judicial ruling. For this reason, it is usually preferable for a mediator who has been involved in a case that moves into arbitration to refer the couple to another mediator-arbitrator who can take a fresh look at the problems from an arbitrator's perspective. When the court examines the matter, it can utilize the decision of the arbitrator along with any new information that appears to affect the best interests of the children involved. In many cases, however, the courts have upheld the arbitrator's recommendation in the absence of any compeling new evidence.

An advisory arbitration award will ultimately become binding under normal circumstances. The difference in practice between advisory and binding arbitration is largely psychological or emotional. Some divorcing couples may wish to feel that they have the option or the freedom to reject the arbitrator's decision and keep the possibility of going to court open, even though they will be aware that the decision is likely to be reinforced by the courts.

When thoroughly explained, arbitration is an attractive alternative for those people who cannot settle their disputes through the courts. The process is not public, affidavits are not required, cases need not be fabricated, "expert" witnesses are not called as advocates for opposing sides, no one is punished nor is there a "winner." Arbitration is, instead, a form of social investigation similar to adoption proceedings or delinquency cases. In none of these procedures nor in divorce mediation are absolute "truths" being sought. (By absolute truths I mean facts that would imply guilt or innocence.) In matters that have to do with relationships between and among family members, a great deal resides in the area of feelings, needs and desires. There *is* no hard evidence as there is in other legal situations. In every case the purpose is to find the best possible remedy for a social problem with the fewest casualties, and with perhaps none at all.

In order to arrive at an arbitrated solution, all relevant information may be used without applying rigorous courtroom standards in resolving what is seen in this context as a social problem. The arbitrator can essentially set his own rules concerning the admissibility of evidence and thus he or she can help prevent the acrimony created by affidavits and the inevitable name-calling therein.

If the arbitrator authorizes reports, for example, from a social worker, and if these are used, the social worker would presumably be available for a hearing or interview. The confidentiality of the source, however, would be respected and use of the social worker as a court witness would be prevented. Cross-examination and rebuttal are permitted and the lawyers would probably be present, but the overall atmosphere is certainly less formal and more flexible than that of the courtroom.

Since the arbitrator has no interest in punishing one party or rewarding another, and since the arbitrator holds the interests of the children to be paramount, he or she is in an ideal position to exercise impartiality. The arbitrator is not employed by either party. He is trained and accredited in the field of human relations. His or her experience is in the area of understanding the web of human action and reaction. As a third party, the arbitrator's vision should be clear enough to see both sides of the dispute and to offer a fair decision. The arbitrator is not, however, a judge. The finding must ultimately be sanctioned by the court.

The use of arbitration to settle marital disputes and facilitate a divorce agreement is in line with a current tendency of the courts to support the use of conciliation services. In addition to the clear benefits for the divorcing couple and their children, there is the further advantage of time. The arbitrated settlement is faster and avoids the substantial time-lags so often involved in getting a case to court. There is less cost and a reduced probability of creating or aggravating conflict, anger and tension.

The following case example illustrates how binding arbitration works:

Mr. and Mrs. Spencer had met at teacher's college. They established a good relationship centered on common goals. They married while still in school. Mrs. Spencer soon had two children, one after the other. After graduation, the Spencers moved from their basically rural surroundings to an urban center where jobs were more plentiful. Their marriage began to deteriorate. Mrs. Spencer accused Mr. Spencer of excessive drinking and inconsiderate, sometimes violent behavior.

During Mrs. Spencer's third pregnancy, marriage counseling was tried, but without positive results. Finally, Mrs. Spencer demanded that her husband move out, and after he had gone, she met a wealthy man who subsequently moved in with her.

Shortly after the appearance of Steven, Mrs. Spencer's live-in companion, the father, Mr. Spencer, was prevented from visiting his children. This resulted in a fist-fight between Mr. Spencer and Steven and, worse, the fight took place in front of the children. A lawyer was then hired by Steven to keep the father away from the children. Needless to say, Mrs. Spencer had no recourse but to side with Steven in order not to place her newly-found relationship in jeopardy. The oldest child, Richard, was obviously upset by the fighting and other disruptions in his life and on the advice of their lawyer, Mrs. Spencer took Richard to a psychiatrist. This was done without the father's knowledge and, in fact, Mrs. Spencer, Steven and the psychiatrist urged Richard to keep the psychiatric visits a secret from Mr. Spencer.

The actions taken by Mrs. Spencer in this case illustrate an interesting and tragic sequence of events. In many custody and visitation disputes the custodial parent, in an effort to either gain custody or prevent visits, may take the child to a psychiatrist to help the child adjust to the situation. The tragedy is that the child through psychiatric therapy is often conditioned to develop a strong alliance with the custodial parent and a serious rift develops with the visiting parent. This approach in therapy is based in part on the recommendation offered in the well-known book, *Beyond the Best Interests of the Child*.[3] Some interpret this as implying that custody be irrevocably awarded to one parent with total authority. It would seem from this, that the non-custodial parent's opportunities to visit would be at the sole discretion of the custodial parent who would make all the decisions for the child. There does not appear to be any empirical research to support this view. The theory that the child will best adjust if the custodial parent makes all the decisions and has total authority is without foundation. As a matter of fact, all the studies point to the fact that when the child sees the visiting parent frequently and when there is a good relationship between the parents, the child adjusts quite well.

Kelly and Wallerstein, who are doing important follow-up research on the effects of divorce on children, report that, "the usual visiting arrangement in which the non-custodial parent takes the children every other weekend appeared to be woefully inadequate." They go on: "The only younger children reasonably content with the visiting situation were those 7- and 8-year-olds visiting two or three times per week, most often pedaling to their father's apartment on a bicycle."[4] Hetherington, Cox and Cox in their study reported similar findings and added that no other support relationship was as valuable for the single parent raising her children as "the continued, positive, mutually supportive relationship of the divorced couple and continued involvement of the father with the child."[5] Rosen, in her discussion of the findings of 92 children of divorce, further corroborates the research findings. "Clinical evidence points strongly to 'free access' being most desirable from the children's point of view. According to what the children themselves said, one source of unhappiness and frustration in children would be alleviated by advising and helping parents to encourage freedom of access between child and non-custodial parent."[6]

In the Spencers' case, Richard received therapy based on the solo parent theory. Following his visits to the psychiatrist, he began to describe Steven as his "psychological" parent while his father, with whom he had had a warm and loving relationship, became his "biological" parent. When questioned about these terms Richard answered that his doctor had explained this to him. Richard also went on to relate that it was very important that he be good to Steven.

Later, I received a letter from Mrs. Spencer's lawyer indicating that there would be a court order to stop all visits between Richard and his father. The lawyer had enclosed a letter from the psychiatrist stating that Richard had a very close and meaningful relationship with his mother and that she provided a great deal of stability for him. The psychiatrist went on to say that Mrs. Spencer and Steven would eventually marry and that as a result, Richard would have a stable family to live with. Further, the psychiatrist felt that any visits between the father and his son would create further conflict between the parents and ultimately Richard would suffer.

The psychiatrist's view is typical of the pronouncements in the same book–that the children are better off having contact exclusively with the custodial parent and should not risk any conflict by seeing the visiting parent. In a recent family law article this point is made . . . "Insofar as it will distort the practical or emotional life of a family, access should be regarded with caution if it contravenes the wishes of the custodial parent."[7]

In the Spencer case, the practice of this theory was made even more harmful because the psychiatrist made his views known to the court without ever seeing the father of the children.

Mr. Spencer agreed that Richard was being traumatized, but he felt his visits upset Mrs. Spencer's companion, Steven, and not his son. Mr. Spencer maintained the view that even though Richard was exposed to a great deal of negative comment about him, the real source of the upset was Steven.

Richard was caught in the middle. He would tell his mother that he didn't want his father to visit, and he would tell his father that he did want the visits. Obviously, the situation was extremely damaging to everyone, but it was particularly damaging to Richard. The problem was escalating rapidly.

Mr. Spencer's lawyer contacted me about the situation and asked if I would be willing to help the family reach an out-of-court solution. After reviewing the situation, I met with both lawyers and explained that the only possible role for me depended on whether or not the parties would agree to binding arbitration. My insistence on binding arbitration was based on the fact that Mrs. Spencer was caught in a situation which she could not resolve by herself. *If* she agreed with her husband, she would alienate Steven.

During an interview with the spouses which was the first time they had spoken face to face in nearly three years, the binding arbitration procedure was outlined. The outline included the fact that the arbitrator's report would have a strong impact on the court. Both Mr. and Mrs. Spencer were very much in favor of the binding approach and the idea that I would be free to control the situation and impose rules and regulations for the eventual betterment of their son.

The Spencers were interviewed separately. Then Richard was interviewed alone and finally Steven. My report imposed a two-part solution. First, Mr. Spencer's visits should be permitted every other weekend leading to overnight stays on alternate weekends. This arrangement, I felt, would provide time to find out whether Mr. Spencer's visits were, in themselves, damaging. This arrangement continued for two months, during which time I continued to see the family as a unit. Steven was invited, but refused to come.

Substantial progress was made. It turned out that Richard was filled with guilt and uncertainty about his role in the situation as a whole. He did not want to lose his father and did not resent his father's visits. In fact, he welcomed them. Richard's teacher notified Mrs. Spencer that Richard was doing better in school and was interacting with the other children. (Such interaction had been previously difficult for him.) It was also noted that he was less defiant with the children in his neighborhood and seemed generally more outgoing and happy. The benefits of the solution were quite apparent to both mother and father who accepted the report and agreed to return as further problems developed. My decision also relieved Mrs. Spencer since it meant she did not have to make the decision herself and go against Steven's wishes.

Binding arbitration *is not* the preferred approach in divorce mediation, especially since there is always a possibility that the arbitrator can make a mistake, but binding arbitration is certainly preferable to the kind of destructive conflict that awaited the Spencers in the courtroom and the emotional danger that would have been done to young Richard if access had been denied to either parent. Court orders are frequently of little help in resolving disputes presented by cases such as this.

In this specific case the arbitrator's report enabled Steven to save face without the resentment inherent in the adversary system. Mrs. Spencer didn't have to support Steven at the hearing because the arbitration report was binding. That meant she had no choice but to go along with the recommendations.

Thus far we have dealt only with the initial decision of a couple to separate and the means of establishing rules governing custody, visitation, and maintenance within a system of divorce mediation. When a divorce is granted, however, time does not stop. Parents continue to be parents and predictably, circumstances can and do change. *After* mediation has taken place and a settlement has been reached, a former spouse may wish to re-open or re-negotiate a prior decision concerning custody or visitation. A job transfer to another city is one example of changed circumstance that might require re-negotiation of visitation rights. Re-marriage by one of the former spouses is another example.

To utilize divorce mediation in changed circumstances (see Figure 2) the procedure is similar to that used in the initial procedure although several alterations are necessary. If the former spouses are able to settle the issue privately and no change in any document is required, the matter can rest. If, however, the courts are to be involved, the couple should meet with the mediator at least briefly. As before, the mediator's role is to try to help the couple in an amicable settlement before it becomes necessary to enter into a court battle.

Figure 2

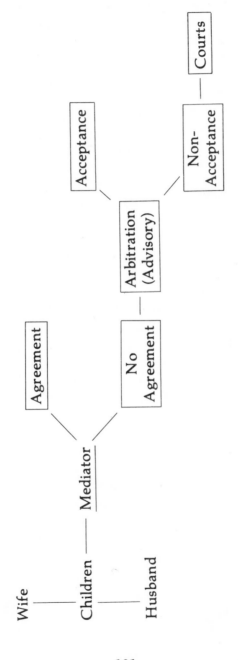

DISPITE RESOLUTION
UNDER CHANGED CIRCUMSTANCES:

Wife — Children — Mediator — Agreement

Mediator — No Agreement — Arbitration (Advisory) — Acceptance

Arbitration (Advisory) — Non-Acceptance — Courts

Husband

The mediator's role in the divorce mediation system is obviously quite different from the lawyer's role. The lawyer has a power conferred on him or her by the individual client. The mediator has the opportunity to persuade the couple to take a fair course of action, but, unlike the lawyer, the mediator is not interested in the best arrangement for an individual client. The mediator seeks the best solution for all concerned, especially the children, and there are no "sides" taken. Mediation and, where necessary, arbitration, has the benefit of permitting creativity and innovation toward constructive solutions.

Spencer and Zammit, in an article published in *The Arbitration Journal*, cite "Family dispute services as making a major contribution . . . by eliminating the concept of fault, by minimizing the adversary nature of familial problems, and by emphasizing self-determination in the resolution of such problems."[8]

The most encouraging thing about divorce mediation is that the families who have tried it are enthusiastic about the way *they themselves* have been able to solve their own problems.

In another similar case, a mother who wanted custody of her five-year-old child was instructed by her lawyer to have her child evaluated at the psychiatric department of a local hospital. Following several sessions, both with the mother and the child, the psychiatrist sent the following letter to the mother's lawyer:

Dear Mr. Evans:

I am writing to you regarding your client, Mrs. Lang, whose 5-year-old daughter, Alice, was referred to our department for a custody evaluation. Alice and her mother have been seen weekly for the past three months. During this time Alice's behavior has improved at home in that she has become less active and more relaxed. Also in school her ability to concentrate has improved. Mrs. Lang seems more relaxed in her relationship with Alice. The improvement is evidenced in that Alice is more secure and has adjusted very well to the marital separation.

Therefore, unless the father's situation has also improved markedly, we would agree that the temporary custody be moved forward to a final custody with mother so that Alice's welfare would be best served in her mother's household. We also recommend that consideration be given to the question of Alice's potential stepfather, Mr. Fredericks, for adopting Alice. We understand that Mrs. Lang is considering re-marriage in the near future. We feel that the adoption will lead to Alice's continuing feelings of security.

I trust this letter will aid you in your efforts to help Alice.

This is another example of how the visiting parent was not included in the therapy or evaluation. In fact he was never asked to participate. When I enquired as to why this happened, the psychiatrist informed me that the mother was dead set against this and furthermore that he concurred with her. He stated his fears that any contact between the parents would be detrimental to Alice.

These kinds of situations make it more imperative that we look at methods of mediation and arbitration to avert the kind of approach illustrated in these two cases.

One of the most important goals of divorce mediation is to facilitate a healthy experience for the child with each of his parents. In many cases where the parents have been involved in an adversarial conflict for a long period of time, the mediator must try and rescue the children from the anger that the parents have for each other. Custodial parents many times will direct the anger toward undermining visitation with the other parent, usually in unclear and subtle ways. The visiting parent may, in reacting to this situation, bring the child back later than agreed. This is a way of dealing with his anger regarding the situation. Because the child is the victim, the mediator must apply all his skill to defuse that situation so that the child has an opportunity for positive contact with each parent.

Chapter Seven

AN ADAPTABLE SYSTEM

The advantage of divorce mediation lies in its flexibility. It would be ideal if one could say, Here are the rules and this is what divorce mediation is and this is how it should be carried out. Such is not the case. Divorce mediation would not be as useful and workable as it is if it had stringent "rules" and a consistent format. There are, certainly, some rules for the mediator-arbitrator, but there is also the quality of flexibility.

No system or method is perfect. Divorce mediation has both failings and problems, but it has proven to be a rational, humane, and successful alternative to the loss, destructive conflict, anger and damage that grow out of adversarial divorce in our society. Divorce mediation solutions may, at times, appear unorthodox in that they don't follow traditional methods of problem solving. Traditionally, long term individual therapy might be suggested. Such long term therapy, however, is not necessarily a feature of divorce mediation.

The clinical literature, whether psychiatric, psychological, sociological or anthropological often presents case studies in a manner suggesting that the specific method being used had been completely thought out and was completely functioning from the start of the specific study. The subjects of the study appear as cogs within the system as they work through the author's procedures. Divorce mediation is a new field. It is continually growing and altering as more families are seen and helped. Divorce mediation is based on dialog–on the give and take between the spouses and among family members, and the persuasive and negotiating abilities of the mediator. In my own experience, I have been shown time and time again that a mediator-arbitrator must be willing to adapt the method to the people and to incorporate new findings in future work.

A case in point was my involvement with the Faulkner family early in the development of the divorce mediation method. Mr. and Mrs. Faulkner had a dual career marriage: he held a managerial position while she designed and sold her own pottery. They had been married eleven years and had two daughters, Kate and Janice. Mr. Faulkner began to have second thoughts about the viability of the marriage, and he determined, finally, that he simply did not love his wife anymore. He began staying out late, drinking heavily, and being generally abusive to his wife. The only sexual contact this couple had as their relationship deteriorated occurred when the husband was drunk. The wife was willing to tolerate all of this behavior just to control the situation and keep the marriage together. She felt that to confront her husband might destroy the marriage completely. She was unable to accept the truth: her husband really didn't love her.

One of the greatest problems in their marriage resulted from the fact that their two daughters were participating in a kind of Olympic training for skating careers. Lessons were never-ending, competition the ruling factor in their lives. Their mother's fondest wish was that they would have successful careers as skaters. She was constantly working with them when not involved in her business. Her husband felt he had been completely shut out of family life. Their problems turned into open hostility with the result that Mrs. Faulkner convinced her husband that they should attend marital therapy sessions. The therapy continued for six months and then stopped abruptly when the husband realized he could not participate in the marriage any further. Nonetheless, he was deeply fond of the two children and was concerned about having reasonable access to them. He had doubts about access because of the demanding skating schedule that their mother had set up.

The couple was referred to me by Mr. Faulkner's attorney, an extremely fair and conciliatory family lawyer. The lawyer realized that going to court on the visitation issue would not be beneficial for the parents or the children and was in favor of a mediated solution. Mrs. Faulkner's counsel was unknown to me, except for his reputation as a tough "adversary" type. During a joint meeting with the lawyers, both were convinced that as a mediator I would not be acting as an advocate for either party. This acceptance was necessary because Mrs. Faulkner's lawyer did not know me and the referral had come from the "other side."

The first joint meeting with the couple was tense. Mrs. Faulkner, an attractive, dark-haired woman with an athlete's slim figure, appeared to be in her early thirties. She was obviously distraught and responded to questions about the children by saying such things as: "This is impossible, I can't believe it. We were so happy, what happened?" Mr. Faulkner was thirty-eight. Balding, but tanned and fit, he carried his age well. He tried to explain to his wife–by appealing to me, as often happens–that emotionally he "couldn't cut this anymore. All I'm interested in right now is the kids. She's just trying to get me to stick it out."

As is often the case where there is still an emotional attachment even though a physical separation has taken place, the spouse wanting to rescue the marriage will vent anger as a way to continue the conflict and thus the relationship. When this becomes all-consuming, individual therapy *is* recommended. It is important during this emotional crisis that the mediation remain focused on what is best for the children. As was evidenced by Mr. Faulkner, he was having a difficult time keeping any objectivity.

It was apparent that we were on the verge of a hysterical argument between two emotional, highly strung people. I had to interject by saying: "We are not here to discuss the past, but to solve the immediate issue of what is best for your daughters. I'd like to know what you both think will be the most beneficial access arrangement–not for either one of you–but for your daughters. Let's think about them, not the past."

Mr. Faulkner's reaction was immediate. "Listen, I've been kept away from my kids ever since this damned skating started, and I'm not going to tolerate any limits on access during separation or divorce!"

Mrs. Faulkner explained–"The lessons are extremely important. If the girls are going to have careers, they have to keep in training all the time and he just can't interrupt that. It's bad enough I have to swallow the idea that he doesn't love me anymore."

As far as I could determine the lines were clearly drawn between them, but once more I asked what was best for the children. Was it better for them to stop skating altogether to satisfy the father, or was it better that their mother's wish for their eventual success make them lose their father's love and attention. I suggested that perhaps it would be a good idea for me to see the girls and find out how *they* felt. In the meantime, I asked the couple to think about the possibility that they might be using the children as wedges against each other.

The meeting with the girls was productive. They seemed fairly well adjusted, but were obviously feeling guilty about their parents' marital problems. I asked them how they felt about seeing their dad, and whether they felt his visits would get in the way of their lessons. Janice, the older girl, responded "We know Dad won't live with us anymore, but we didn't mean to do anything to make him mad. We want to see him a lot." Kate was unwilling to say anything at first. She sat across from me with her legs crossed and played with the figure skating pin that she wore. Finally, she blurted out: "We want to skate too, but we love him!" It seemed clear that both girls were upset about the breakup of their parents. They didn't really want to stop skating and they didn't want to choose between their parents.

During the second interview with Mr. and Mrs. Faulkner, I explained that in my opinion the best interests of the children were not being served by pitting skating against visiting. Privately, I was aware that Mrs. Faulkner was insisting on the prime importance of practice and lesson time as a method of controling the situation and making Mr. Faulkner come to her. He on the other hand, was demanding unlimited access in order to assert the rights he felt he had lost. After discussing my recommendation with them, this couple was able to see, for the time being at least, that their marital problems couldn't be permitted to tear the children apart, and a mediated agreement was worked out to the satisfaction of both of them. Mr. Faulkner would move out. Mrs. Faulkner would have custody of both girls, but he would have reasonable access. Between them, "reasonable access" was defined as one evening per week and overnight visits on alternate weekends. Religious, statutory, and school holidays would be split between them. Mr. Faulkner would not undermine the idea of skating nor would he prevent the daughters from minimal necessary practicing when they were with him for extended periods of time. For her part, the mother would refrain from undermining her husband's authority over the children, nor would she unreasonably deny the access terms of the agreement.

As a negotiated settlement that avoided litigation this was acceptable to both spouses, but I could see that Mrs. Faulkner was still involved emotionally with her husband. I offered her a referral to a psychiatrist who could assist her in disengaging from him. She accepted the referral, and the family was satisfied that a beneficial agreement had been hammered out.

Within a month, as I later found out, Mr. Faulkner met another woman with whom he established a friendship. She was present on many occasions when his children were visiting. When Mrs. Faulkner heard about this she complained that the children simply weren't ready for this kind of thing. She threatened not to allow any visits at all. Initially, Mr. Faulkner promised not to have his girlfriend with him when the children were around. Unfortunately, however, this promise was not kept.

About three months after the mediation agreement was signed, Mr. Faulkner telephoned me in great distress with the news that his wife and children had disappeared. Frantic, he had called her friends and was surprised and annoyed to learn that they already knew she was away. All they could say was that she had gone on holiday with no specified date of return. They did not know where she or the children were. I reassured him that I would do everything possible to discover their whereabouts. He went on to discuss his fears that they might not return. He was obviously in a state of panic. I asked him to come to the office while I tried to locate them.

I immediately telephoned Mrs. Faulkner's lawyer and after being put on "hold" for what seemed like hours, I finally got through to him. When I explained that we were trying to locate his client, he let me know in no uncertain terms that he had counseled his client to "kidnap" the children. He knew where they were, they were safe, but he felt it was time that Mr. Faulkner understood that his client would only permit visiting on her terms.

I was shocked not only by what the lawyer told me but how in fact he felt about the situation. It was as if he were speaking of closing a real estate deal–everything was in order and there was nothing for us to worry about. Finally, he went on to reassure me that when he was a boy his parents took him out of school when they vacationed in the south prior to the Christmas holiday. He asked, "So what's the big deal with this situation?"

At this point I realized that mediation would be to no avail, unless this lawyer could be convinced how damaging his conduct was to all concerned. I immediately urged him to attend a meeting so that we could get to the bottom of the situation. He seemed responsive to this, almost as if he thought, "Now we'll get some action." In effect, he was doing the best one could expect of an advocate in the adversarial system. In his view there was no difference between a criminal case and one dealing with a father's wishes to see his children.

By meeting with the lawyers once more, I was able to persuade them that using threatening letters and encouraging disappearances were extremely detrimental to the children's interests and that further, such action would prevent any positive relationship between the parents. After three days, Mrs. Faulkner's attorney phoned to report that his client was prepared to discuss the situation with her husband. For the time being, however, the children would stay away from home. I asked for a five-way interview to include the spouses, the lawyers and myself. The meeting began with a great deal of shouting between the lawyers who accused each other of coercion and unethical conduct. The parents shouted about "loose women" and kidnapping. The tension relaxed after this emotional outburst. The lawyers and the spouses responded to the mediator, the only person in the room who did not enter into the arguments. It was possible to convince Mrs. Faulkner and her attorney to bring the children home and to negotiate a four-to-six-session family contract for therapy.

The Faulkner family met with a therapist for about three months. Finally, they were able to see how destructive it was for the mother to use access to the children as a way of preventing the father from leading his own life and how unreasonable it was for him to impose his own rules about company during visits without consulting his wife. The original agreement was reaffirmed, but with the added proviso that if either one did not live up to the agreement, they were required to call the mediator before any action was taken–legal or otherwise.

Emotionally distraught or bitter people bent on retaliation are seldom ready to resolve practical issues by themselves before emotional realities are faced. The mediator's role in such a situation is primarily to prevent damage to the children while assisting in the resolution of such practical problems as visitation. The emotional side of the question might be handled by referrals, (such as to a psychiatrist) but it is not the mediator's primary goal.

This case taught me a great deal about the mediation process. It clearly pointed out that mediation agreements need to specify that any breakdown in the terms of the agreement should be referred back to the mediator before the adversarial system is brought into play. The intensely inflammatory potential of this case when the attorneys became involved was alarmingly real. Regarding the lawyers, the behavior of Mr. Faulkner's counsel surprised me. After the case was resolved, he explained that at first he was unable to tolerate Mrs. Faulkner's behavior from a purely emotional standpoint. His reaction was complicated, though, by the fact that he was trying to be conciliatory in the pending divorce proceedings, but the "other side" was "walking all over him." There is little to be said for Mrs. Faulkner's lawyer; his behavior was plainly unethical, but he said he was just protecting his client's interests: "All's fair in war."

Although it is usual for us to believe that attorneys do not become emotionally involved in their cases and look only at the legal facts at issue, it is remarkable how easy it is for emotional legal involvement to develop in marital disputes. There are many conciliatory divorce lawyers, but they are hampered by the very existence of an adversarial system that permits a tough attorney to "walk all over them." In a sense there is a paradox. When a good lawyer, one who has the children's interest at heart and who uses conciliatory methods through negotiation, for example, is up against the adversarial-type lawyer, he will, perhaps, lose ground with his client. This is further complicated by the fact that lawyers gain a reputation by "winning," and not by being conciliatory. The conciliatory method does work when both opposing lawyers are conciliatory in their approach. Then the results are beneficial to all concerned. The adversarial system is often frustrating to moderate lawyers and usually leads to a situation where it becomes necessary to retaliate in kind.

Adversarial divorce law is rife with such inequalities. For example, there are no legal provisions for the rights of grandparents in custody cases. In legal access terms, it simply is not possible to specify that grandparents have any rights at all. This is a common dilemma that is tragic for older people who suddenly can't see their grandchildren as often as they once did, or who are completely denied access because the parents are divorced. This situation is equally tragic for the children who have a special relationship with all their grandparents.

Before becoming involved in the next case discussed, I, like many professionals as well as non-professionals, paid little attention to the role of the grandparents in divorce. This case illustrates their importance and it serves as a further example of the adaptability of the divorce mediation system.

Mrs. Gordon contacted me to help her solve a problem she was having with her former husband and his parents. As she explained the situation to me, her former in-laws were responsible for the breakdown of the marriage. She believed her in-laws had convinced her husband that she wasn't "right" for him. As part of the divorce settlement, a result of contested action, she won custody of their son. There was a stipulated provision for overnight access to the child for the husband on alternate weekends.

Mrs. Gordon's difficulty was that she did not want her son to visit her former in-laws. In her own words: "Why should I be nice to them? They destroyed my marriage." She had no legal recourse to prevent the visits, but felt I might be able to help her mediate a solution. I responded that as mediator my role couldn't be to determine the truth or falsity of her perception of the grandparents' role in the marriage breakdown. I did add my view that if the parents were able to control their son (Mr. Gordon) to that extent, he must be remarkably weak. I wondered whether, considering the conditions, she had a worthwhile marriage in the first place. In order to help her find out what might be the best course of action, I asked to see the boy himself. Mrs. Gordon readily agreed.

Her son came to my office, sat down, looked around vacantly and decided not to talk. I let him continue his silence for a few minutes and then told him that his mother was having a problem that he might be able to help solve. This approach seemed to startle him a bit–it was obviously difficult for him not to respond on this level. After explaining the problem, I asked how he felt about the situation. He told me that he liked all four of his grandparents. "I know my mom doesn't like me to see Grandpa and Grandma Gordon though."

Armed with this information, I met with the mother once more and asked if the boy's happiness was important to her. She readily agreed that it was. I explained that perhaps it was possible that the question here was not whether her husband's parents interfered in the marriage, but whether they had anything positive to offer her son. According to the boy, he liked his grandparents and didn't want to stop seeing them. As soon as Mrs. Gordon was able to separate her anger over the marriage breakup from the welfare of her son, she became rational enough to understand that it was, in fact, beneficial for him to see them.

Although Mrs. Gordon still wasn't completely convinced that the relationship would stay within reasonable bounds, it was decided to have a joint meeting with the grandparents.

The senior Gordons initiated the discussion by letting us know they loved the grandchild dearly and would do anything to help out in the situation. The grandfather particularly tried to impress his daughter-in-law that they were sorry about the marital breakup and wanted to remain friends with her. He went on to relate that the grandson was doing very well and that she should be very proud of him. While Grandfather was talking, it became clear that Mrs. Gordon was not as angry or as resentful as I had thought. She was quite supportive and most of the interview was conducted in a positive manner. It was almost as if everyone was relieved at having the opportunity to talk openly between and among themselves. The most important aspect of the meeting was their face-to-face encounter without having to communicate through their lawyers in an indirect and impersonal manner. It was fascinating to see how Mrs. Gordon related to her in-laws. Soon after the interview started she referred to them as "Mom and Dad." It was almost as if all the previous accusations, name-calling, and so on had never happened.

In the four-way interview that followed, a mediated arrangement was worked out whereby the grandparents agreed they would not undermine Mrs. Gordon's authority in any way and she in turn would not disparage them to her son. The end result was that Mrs. Gordon's son would feel free to have affectionate relationships with them all.

As it turned out, this solution was workable and beneficial because the grandfather was a particularly responsible person.

The child, in fact, had better care from his grandparents than from his father.

The rather painless solution worked out by this family makes one wonder what might have happened had the situation been handled in an adversarial manner. The grandparents had no legal rights, of course, but if their son was as weak as the facts seemed to indicate, litigation for increased access or custody might have been started. The result probably would have been alienation and a great deal of financial hardship for everyone. Mediation, in this case, despite the fact that it did not accomplish what Mrs. Gordon had originally wanted, was highly successful. It prevented the inevitable guilt and crossed loyalties that the child would have come to feel in a court case.

There are, of course, situations where grandparents become overly involved and in fact contribute toward destructive family situations. In one such case the parents were fairly amicable in terminating their marriage until the maternal grandparents decided to make sure that their daughter was not going to let her husband get away with anything. The daughter was very dependent, one of the reasons the couple decided to separate in the first place. In essence her parents were just continuing the same pattern of becoming overly involved in their daughter's situation.

The interesting side of it for me, as a mediator, was the fact that the daughter asked me if I could help her keep her parents out of the divorce. When I contacted the grandparents they were angry, refused to come in for an appointment and told me that I was making things worse. They obviously had a need to stay in the situation and the more conflict for the daughter, the more they felt needed. Although we were all convinced that the grandparents were getting in the way of settling the dispute, we were impotent in trying to get them to be helpful by staying out of the situation. The couple finally settled their dispute but the situation was drawn out in a way that was harmful and difficult to change because the grandparents were simply not interested in getting involved in a constructive way. It should be noted that they did not do this deliberately, as they actually felt they were doing what was best for their "little girl."

In another situation involving extended family, an older couple in their late sixties was referred for mediation counseling by one of their married daughters. There were two married daughters who had children and lived near their parents. The marriage had been an unhappy one for a number of years. The parents had decided not to divorce, for the sake of the children. When I interviewed the parents, Mr. and Mrs. Johnston, they spent the whole time discussing how terrible each of them was in relation to their children. The daughters had sided with their mother and were doing whatever they could to put pressure on their father so that he would not leave their mother. They had even kept the grandchildren away from their father when he announced he was moving out of the house. The sons-in-law felt that their wives were creating more problems by getting involved. In fact, they felt their own marriages were being affected by their in-law situation.

It was the daughter who hired a lawyer for her mother and was instigating litigation as a way to threaten and control her father. After a number of sessions which included the parents and the children, we were able to open the lines of communication and although not resolving the problems, the daughters became aware of how their involvement was harmful to any resolution of the problem between their parents. Again, the children thought they were doing the right thing by getting involved at that level and only "wanted to keep their parents together." This case, as well as others, points out the need to have a mediator talk to all the relevant members of the family.

Without a doubt, amicable mediation is not only possible when an atmosphere of rational action is created, but usually it is preferable to arbitration in either a voluntary or compulsory form. All three methods are far better than litigation.

Sometimes, particularly when the adversarial system has already been engaged, arbitration is the only workable solution to disputes short of court action. This is especially true when one of the spouses simply will not recognize that his or her behavior is damaging to the children.

Impartiality is often mentioned as the prime objective of psychological investigation, and this is necessary in divorce mediation so far as personalities are concerned. In some cases, though, it is extremely difficult not to take sides on the issues. Here, the mediator's experience, judgment, and fact-finding abilities are crucial in making proper and fair evaluations.

At first, the case of the Traynor family seemed unusual to me. After many similar cases, however, I now regard it as a model for the use of arbitration in the divorce dispute resolution method.

The Traynors had been married for fifteen years during which time two sons, Robert and Steven, were born. At the time of the divorce the older child, Robert, was fourteen and Steven was twelve. When I became involved in the case, Mr. Traynor had a terrible employment record. He had bounced from job to job and relied on his wife to keep the family going financially. Mrs. Traynor resented this situation. Her method of expressing resentment was to restrict their sex life to a once a month maximum where she was never the aggressor, thus keeping her husband in a very defensive and uncertain position sexually. This type of situation does not usually continue too long before help is sought or breakdown occurs.

Mrs. Traynor decided that the marriage was over for her, a decision that her husband could not accept. Nevertheless, they drew up a legal separation agreement. For the time being the mother had custody of the two boys, granting the husband liberal access to them. In order to visit, the husband had to commute from a nearby city where he had found what seemed to be his first really steady job in nearly six years.

The separation had continued for almost a year. It was a period during which the wife received some financial support at first and then no support at all from her husband. The elder son, Robert, expressed a wish to live with his father. Since the boy apparently wanted it, and since Mrs. Traynor was trying to

116

hold down a job and maintain the two boys at the same time, she agreed. There is no doubt that she loved her son, but she was aware that her husband was attached to both children. It seemed fair for one boy to live with his father, so long as she could have him visit with her. What appeared to be an equitable arrangement was worked out between them: Robert would visit with his mother while Steven visited his father.

Problems began to develop, however, when Steven returned from his father's home. He became sullen and unmanageable, his school work began to suffer, and he became increasingly critical of his mother. Mrs. Traynor was admittedly incapable of dealing with these symptoms, so she went with him to a family therapy clinic for assistance. During this critical time, her husband began writing to her. The following is an example:

Dear L_____,
It certainly was good to have Stevie here for Thanksgiving. It was a shame that you had to visit your mother then, I hope she's better. I explained to Stevie and Bobby that your mother was sick and it was very important for you to be with her even though it was Thanksgiving.
We had a lot of fun and it looks like I'll be able to take both boys to the Bahamas as I promised.
Stevie is very happy when he's here. It really is a shame that they have to be separated like this, and I think we should work out something so that they can be together all the time. Bobby's doing very well in school and likes the new bike I gave him.
Please tell Stevie we are thinking about him all the time.
Yours affectionately,

B _____

Mrs. Traynor continued receiving similar letters. The husband also started writing to Steven:

Dear Stevie,
Boy, didn't we have a great time at the game! Bobby and I do things like this all the time, and we always miss having you with us.
Bobby thinks about you all the time, he even woke up last night

thinking what fun it would be to have you here all the time.

I haven't forgotten about the other guinea pig I promised you, but maybe we could make a whole family sometime with Bobby's two and your old one and your new one. Anyway, I'm sending along the dollar I forgot to give you.

We can't wait to see you again, so ask your mom when it would be convenient for her to let you come, even if Bobby can't stay with her. We'll do great things together.

> *Love,*
> *Dad & Bobby*

Dear L_____ ,

It's too bad it wasn't convenient to have Bobby over last weekend, but I took advantage of the situation and took both boys to the hockey game. Stevie was very interested and maybe he should try out for a team next year. There's one near here, and I'll see if he can qualify. Your new job must be very demanding if you have to work weekends!

I really think that the boys are happiest when they are together and I believe that they should be together with me, because I am willing to spend my time with them and take them places. You don't seem to want to get back together which would be the best thing for all. It just won't be possible for you to care for Stevie like I can.

I'm sure that if you think about this you'll see that I'm right.

> *Yours affectionately,*

> *B _____*

Mrs. Traynor had notified her lawyer regarding the letters and, according to her, the lawyer was so incensed and outraged that he told her the letters constituted an attempt to intimidate her. Instead of answering the letters, Mrs. Traynor filed for divorce. Her husband responded by petitioning for custody of Steven. Mrs. Traynor based her divorce on separation and irreconcilable differences. Mr. Traynor filed affidavits to the effect that she was an unfit mother.

The following excerpts from the affidavit point out the harmful aspects of proceeding with litigation in the present adversarial system. The fault basis was clearly the rationale for which the accusations of a most severe and painful nature were made by Mr. Traynor and his lawyer. How does one respond to being called an unfit and irresponsible mother? The only avenue, of course, is to hit back harder when you are fighting to keep your child.

"The Respondent does not provide a loving home for Steven. For trifling errors she responds by screaming, shouting and throwing things.

I am gainfully employed and provide a comfortable home for our eldest son, Bob, where love and affection, not screaming fits are prevalent.

It is my contention that the Respondent is unfit to care for Steve, and that he should be placed in my custody along with his brother."

At the husband's instigation, the question of custody was ordered into arbitration by the court. He was insistent that the arbitration be binding, feeling sure that anyone could see that he was right. The court order stipulated that both divorce and custody proceedings be halted pending the outcome.

The husband's lawyer contacted me to act as arbitrator. After the usual meeting with both attorneys I scheduled a joint interview with the spouses.

Mrs. Traynor came into my office first, closely followed by her husband. She was nicely and neatly dressed, but she was obviously harried, overworked, and overweight. Her clothes fit in a way that suggested her weight gain was recent. Her speech was nervous and up-and-down in tone as we introduced each other. Her husband was almost the complete reverse: comfortably round, soft spoken, very "up front" and "honest" it seemed. Both of them sat down, the husband taking the seat opposite me and Mrs. Traynor shifting her chair slightly to my right. I explained that we were meeting to outline the rules of binding arbitration, that except for this meeting the information I gathered would be made available to the court in their determination of the custody of the children.

I further stated that my role was to determine the best

interests of the children, not to find out who was at fault for causing the marriage breakdown. Therefore, I was not interested in talking about past occurrences in their lives, even though some information would undoubtedly come to me regarding the state of their married life. This outline was acceptable to both spouses. Normally, the initial interview would have continued to define such things as further procedures and agreement on meeting schedules. However, Mr. Traynor decided to tell us both, appealing to my reason, as he said, that it really was in the best interests of both children to live with him. His wife was "the best mother in the world," but she simply wasn't able to care for both sons at the same time. He contended that the boys should be together, and he was capable of providing what they needed. All of this was given in a very soft spoken tone of voice. To Mr. Traynor, this was a clear-cut case that couldn't help but go *his* way.

The methods used by the divorce arbitrator are not unlike the fact-finding procedures used in labor disputes, delinquency cases, or adoption proceedings. After explaining this to the couple, the necessary releases and permission to see the boys individually were obtained. The first step in the investigation was to see the spouses separately. Mrs. Traynor's interview was first, because of the husband's work schedule. She didn't think she was doing a particularly good job in handling Steven, although since going to therapy things seemed to improve a great deal. She told me that she believed that the discipline problems she was experiencing stemmed to some extent from her husband's treatment of the boy when he was visiting. He was permitted to do anything he wanted, his father constantly promised or gave him things, and continually suggested he would be better off living with him. Steven had reported to her that his father would say things like, Look at all I've done for you, don't you think you should come to live with me?

According to Mrs. Traynor, "I might not be the best mother going, but I'm trying hard, I love both my sons, but I won't be blackmailed." She was certainly willing to fight the custody petition, partially due to the anxiety and anger produced by the letters she and Steven had received (which she had saved and gave to me). Her decision to fight, even though it would be a great financial strain, was sealed by the charges contained in her husband's affidavit.

During Mr. Traynor's interview, the same soft-spoken, righteous attitude prevailed. There was little trace of anxiety, no guilt, but deep resentment over the separation. He was absolutely certain that he was correct in what he wanted. It was only considered unfortunate that by starting divorce proceedings his wife made it necessary for him to sue for custody. It was up to me to determine how to convince her of the best course of action.

Before seeing Steven, I obtained a report from the family therapy clinic that Mrs. Traynor and Steven had attended. During therapy, Mr. Traynor had apparently demanded to be interviewed and he was gladly seen, although at the time the therapists were not sure of the immediate relevance of seeing him. Their report stated in part:

"Mrs. Traynor brought Steven here explaining that he was having trouble sleeping and his marks were dropping off at school. He was difficult to discipline at home, and had little contact with his peers. It was apparent to us that a great many of the boy's problems were caused by the strain of his parent's separation. We began a course of relaxation exercises for him, talked about the separation, and reassured him that none of it was his fault. We assured him further that both his mother and father loved him and they would try to do what was best for him. We saw Steven eight times over two months, and his behavior showed rapid improvement both at home and at school. We also spoke to Mrs. Traynor, and it is our opinion that she is under a great deal of emotional and financial pressure, but there is nothing wrong with her parenting abilities.

"Mr. Traynor was seen twice. He is a persuasive person; he tried to convince us that it would be best for Steven to live with him and the other son. It is our opinion that Mr. Traynor harbors deep resentment about the separation, wants his wife to return to him, and will use any means to accomplish what he 'knows to be right'."

The information contained in this report made interviewing Steven more productive than it might otherwise have been. He did have a marked tendency to be sullen, yet after we had made some small talk, he finally told me that his father really wanted him to come and live in the city with his brother; that his father constantly told him it would be better for him. The father promised trips, hockey equipment, "lots of things." The boy told me further that he didn't find therapy bad at all, had made friends at school to play with, and wanted to stay with his mother. He didn't like the idea that his mother had to work so much, although he was happy at the babysitter's home for an hour until she got home, because the sitter had a son and they played together. Steven didn't want to leave his mother, yet he also wanted to see his father and brother often. He was still fairly sure that something he had done created all the marital problems, but he didn't know what it was.

Seeing Robert was a revelation. He had some of his father's soft-spoken manner, but a very definite personality of his own. There was no problem beginning a conversation with him. He was obviously concerned about his parents and wanted to help. When I asked him about his mother, he said, "My mother's O.K. I like going there to visit."

At this point I was formulating a fairly clear idea of my arbitration report. However, an arbitrator, far more than a mediator, must be absolutely certain of his facts before making a decision. I asked for another joint meeting with the spouses, where I went over some of my findings. Aware that things were not going his way, Mr. Traynor began showing shock and indignation.

Regarding the clinic, his opinion was that the therapists were more interested in his wife than his son. Moreover, he felt that school improvement had to do with *his* giving Steven the affection he needed, affection that he did not receive at home. His quiet demeanor began to deteriorate, and before leaving he blurted out, "If she could only see that we should get back together, all of this wouldn't have happened. It's not my fault!"

Mrs. Traynor told me that she wasn't at all interested in reconciliation; what she did want was to get a divorce, live in peace with her son, let her husband have access to him in a reasonable manner, be able to see Robert in return, and re-establish her own life without harassment.

The issues were clear here. As an arbitrator it was difficult not to take sides. In my mind, it was obvious that Mr. Traynor wanted to return to the marriage, and was willing to use Steven as a means of extorting Mrs. Traynor's compliance. Mrs. Traynor, on the other hand, could not bring herself to enter the marriage again, and she was unwilling to be coerced. Many therapists will say that personalities do not play a part in their treatment. Even as an impartial arbitrator, though, it was impossible not to admire Mrs. Traynor's strength.

On the day after this joint interview, I received a registered letter from Mr. Traynor telling me that my services as an arbitrator were no longer required, because I was "obviously unreasonably biased." I phoned his lawyer about this letter and the lawyer told his client that it was not possible to fire a court-appointed arbitrator, especially in view of the fact that he, himself, had insisted on the procedure and entered into a joint agreement with his wife. The lawyer was fired. Although Mr. Traynor's second and third lawyers also attempted to fire me, I went ahead with the report the court had asked for and to which both parties had originally agreed. The report was simple and to the point, backed by the file of information I had compiled:

"It is my recommendation as arbitrator in this case that custody of Steven Traynor remain with his mother, Mrs. L. Traynor of _____ City. Further, it is my recommendation that the natural father, Mr. B. Traynor of _____ should have reasonable access to Steven in the form of alternate weekends, subject to Mrs. Traynor having equal visitation rights with their other son, Robert.

"Mr. Traynor's access is to be strictly subject to the

requirement that he refrain from undermining his estranged wife's authority regarding the discipline of Steven
and that Mr. Traynor refrain from attempting to convince
either Steven or Mrs. Traynor that Steven should live with
Mr. Traynor."

This arbitrated decision was carried out by the court, and
access was set up with the listed stipulations. This was hardly an
amicable settlement for Mr. Traynor. I received no response
whatever to my offer of a referral for him to a therapist who
might be able to help with his emotional life.

This, of course, was understandable in view of the fact that
I had supported his wife's position in the matter of custody. This
case illustrates the difficult role the mediator must play. After
all, the goal is to try to help the family make their own responsible decisions and not have a decision imposed on them.

Mr. and Mrs. Traynor went on to use the adversarial
system to conclude their divorce. Since Mrs. Traynor was not
receiving any financial support from her husband in any case,
and since she saw the question of financial support as yet
another attempt by her husband to stay involved with her,
money did not become an issue.

After the divorce was concluded, I was contacted by Mr.
Traynor's lawyer who admitted quite frankly that he felt there
was something odd about Mr. Traynor's behavior from the start
of the custody proceedings. He was relieved that the case had
been handled in arbitration since he was convinced that, given
his client's emotional state, persuasive personality and the sheer
power of money, Mr. Traynor had stood a fair chance of winning
custody within the adversarial system. He went on to echo my
own thoughts by saying that he thought this would have been
intensely destructive for Steven as well as for everyone else
involved in the case.

No doubt, Mr. Traynor felt he was doing what was best. It
was obvious to everyone but him that he was not dealing with
the reality of his wife's unwillingness to return to him. The
arbitrator must try to point out this kind of attitude but his

primary role is to establish a structure that prevents damage to the children.

When children are "at risk," the mediator must consider their interests paramount and this is naturally difficult for the parent who does not get what he wants, regardless of whether it is custody or an increase in visitation rights. The sad part of this case was the fact that the way in which the legal aspects were carried out left the parents and the children scarred for a long time.

The cases presented in this chapter show the adaptability of mediation and/or voluntary or binding arbitration, and illustrate the limitations and problems that the arbitrator can and often does face. The advantage of divorce mediation lies in its flexibility. It would be ideal if one could say, Here are the rules and this is what divorce mediation is and this is how it should be carried out. Such is not the case. Divorce mediation would not be as useful and workable as it is if it had stringent "rules" and a consistent format. There are, certainly, some rules for the mediator-arbitrator, but there is also the quality of flexibility. One attempts not to take sides, for example, but the interests of the children *are* paramount and when those interests demand taking sides, as the Traynor case showed, then the flexibility of the divorce mediation method comes into play.

In the following chapter we will look at child custody in more detail. It is in this area of family disputes that the children most often suffer. It is in this area that the mediator-arbitrator can play an important role.

Chapter Eight

CHILD CUSTODY: A LEGAL LOTTERY WITH NO WINNERS

*It is paradoxical that lawyers who are hired to represent children find themselves
going beyond the role of lawyering and for the most part find themselves
functioning as mediators. They meet at times with parents, the parents' lawyers,
the children themselves and all others who are relevant to the dispute.*

The Oxford English dictionary defines a "lottery" as:
"Arrangements for distributing prizes by chance among pur-
chasers of tickets;" and as "Chance, issue of events as determined
by chance."

During the past few years, North Americans have taken to
lotteries with a vengeance.[1] Millions of ticket holders await the
results of the wheel of chance with eager anticipation. Although
cynical, it is not unfair to use the metaphor of the lottery to
describe child custody procedures. The players and their roles in
our not-so-mythical lottery are as follows: the lawyers who
handle the litigation and try to narrow the odds for each
respective player–on one side the mother and on the opposite
side the father; the psychiatrists in their role as "expert witness"–each supporting sometimes opposing views for their
client; the judge who has the difficult and often painful task of
pulling a winning ticket which will decide the fate of the child;
the parents–one of whom will win and the other will lose–and
last, the child, who is awarded as the grand prize to the not-so-
lucky ticket holder.

The oddsmakers will tell you, even before the wheel of chance is spun, that mothers have a far better chance in this game than fathers. The reasons for this lie in the legal system and are due to the so-called "Tender Years Doctrine." As a result of this doctrine, custody disputes which involve younger children almost always end with mother preference being upheld. We will explore the "Tender Years Doctrine" later in this chapter.

The role of the expert witness–usually a psychiatrist–is to support the view of one of the parties. Both parties may have one or more expert witnesses as part of the lawyer's "team" and each tries to narrow the odds. The judges who must choose often feel ill-equipped to deal with such a difficult process. They sometimes wonder whether the adversary system is, in fact, the right method for dealing with this kind of situation. When the decision is finally made, there are no real winners. The demeaning litigation process that preceded the verdict has left the families scarred, often for life.

The damage is understandable only when one looks at the charges and counter-charges made in the process–a process that tries to prove that each loving parent is unfit and unworthy of parenting. The end result of the custody dispute puts the custodial parent in complete control, and this the law legitimizes through the power and authority that it vests in the custodial parent. As previously mentioned, this is known as the "Beyond Best Interests Doctrine." Is it surprising that these cases come back time and again for litigation on matters of visiting or further charges of unfit parenting? We have laws that prevent the buying and selling of children, laws that make child labor illegal, laws that punish those who abuse children. A good many of our laws recognize that children are not owned by their parents, but sadly, the laws, doctrines and precedents of child custody still result in the child being regarded as a chattel–a chattel who, like a house or furniture, will be awarded to the most virtuous parent.

To have a real appreciation of the system, one must look back in history at the development of child custody laws. Early Common Law, as well as English and Roman Dutch Law, regarded the father's right to custody as superior to that of the mother. This, naturally, had to do with the historic status of women: if women were owned by their husbands, so of course, were the children.

"Under the doctrine of natural rights, children were considered property, and a father could exercise complete control over them. His authority was supreme; he could sell them for profit or even order them put to death. During the first century, however, Emperor Constantine decreed that infanticide was prohibited, and this became the first major limitation of parental rights."[2]

The shift toward mother preference was influenced by the doctrine of *Parens patriae* which gave the courts authority to protect and award custody of young children. The awarding of young children to their mothers became part of British common law and eventually became part of statutory provisions in American Law. Over the years and even now, maternal preference has continued to rely on the "Tender Years Doctrine." Many of the reasons for mother preference have to do with faulty assumptions based on maternal instinct and values that are not supported by research. Recently, another change has taken place. The "Tender Years Doctrine" is being challenged as parental roles become more blurred. The Equal Rights Amendment, the women's movement in general and the willingness of fathers to become more involved with their children have all contributed to changing interpretations. Another factor affecting change is the desire of some women to share the responsibility of raising children with their ex-husbands. Many solo parents, both men and women, find child-rearing difficult without the co-operation of the other parent. This attitude change is particularly significant when one realizes that almost 50 percent of the labor force is made up of working women. Moreover, many divorced couples have experienced financial strain making it necessary for both to work. It seems only sensible that many children whose parents are working be involved in more than one child care support system. The *quality* rather than quantity of parental time highlights the disparity of maternal or paternal preference in child custody disputes. In short, a child needs both parents, and single parents often need the freedom shared parenting can offer.

Consider the advantages of sensible parenting arrangements compared to the custody battle. According to Joseph Epstein, "If custody is contested and the father happens to win, there is only one way for him to go: he must prove his wife either an emotional cripple or a moral leper and, should he wish to maximize his chances, preferably both."[3] In such a battle, of course, the mother must also try to prove the father unfit. The accusations and counter accusations are destroying. It is all done with the idea of "winning," but no one wins.

There is a lack of research confirming single father competence in the area of parenting, but five studies reviewed by Orthner and Lewis[4] all point to the father's ability to handle the parental role. Fathers appear to handle the parenting role without much difficulty. Orthner and Lewis go on to say:

"In conclusion, the authors [of the five studies] recognize that each case of disputed child custody must be examined on its own merits. But from the evidence presented in this paper, it is hoped that courts will weigh the facts of each case more carefully without the prejudice of presumptions regarding mother and father competence. This research is not intended to swing the legal pendulum toward fathers or toward any assumption that all fathers should be presumed capable of rearing children. Some men may not make competent single fathers; some women may not make competent single mothers. In many cases, both parents are quite capable of being competent single parents. Contested custody cases are often the most difficult matters for judges. But each case must be examined at a full evidentiary hearing on its merits. It is of paramount concern to the children involved that their parents be judged on their own abilities and not on the legacy of out-dated notions of parental competence."

In Rosen's study of ninety-two children of divorced

parents, in relation to the sex of the custodial parent, it was found that there was no significant difference existing between the two groups (mother custody and father custody) on any measures of the child's adjustment. Furthermore, when the sex of the child and the age at the time of the divorce are analyzed, no significant relationship emerged.[5] It would appear from Rosen's study that any automatic choice of custodial parent based on gender has no supporting evidence. This is an important consideration because many custody battles arise from the "Tender Years Doctrine" and the assumption that the mother has preference.

If one accepts the current trend in custody disputes–that decisions are to be made not on maternal preference but on the merits of each individual case–then we must recognize the impossible task of the courts in deciding custody disputes. In trying to determine the best interest of the child, after weighing the evidence from each parent, the court may feel it advantageous to interview the child and consider the child's preference in the custody dispute. The child may be considered a witness when either parent, in trying to further their case, would call the child as a witness. The child would be examined and cross-examined in an open court room where a judge would have the opportunity to observe the child under oath. This would help form his opinion regarding the child's real preference. A number of questions immediately come to mind. What are the psychological effects of having the child choose between his parents? How much of the child's testimony is influenced by parental pressure? Does the child have the capacity to testify, and if so, what are the competency standards for making this determination?

In the matter of parental influence, Stanley vs. Stanley* is an interesting recent case discussed by authors Siegal and Hunley.[6] The father of a thirteen-year-old boy sought to have custody of the child changed from the mother to himself. In spite of the

*The names in the following three cases have been changed to preserve their confidentiality.

mother's motion for a continuance, the hearing began a week after the boy had returned from a six-week trip with his father. The trial court honored the preference expressed by the child to live with his father; however, the appellate court vacated the order, holding that the denial of the mother's request for a continuance was in error. It acknowledged the importance of the preference of a thirteen-year-old child, but also realized that this particular preference was clouded by the influence of a recent vacation. The appellate court stated:

We are considering a child whose testimony was taken at the end of a summer which began with a gift of a motorcycle and ended with a custody hearing intentionally scheduled immediately upon return from a long vacation in the father's motor home. There is too great a probability that long exposure to the father during vacation as distinguished from normal working life, coupled with excessive material indulgence has tainted the boy's testimony as to preference.

In such a case, the preference of the child is not entitled to the great weight which it otherwise might warrant. There are many instances where the child is coached by the parents.

In another case, Lloyd vs. Lloyd,[7] the ten-year-old child stated, in chambers with the judge, that he preferred to live with his father. On being further questioned concerning his reasons, the child said that he did not think he would get a college education otherwise, adding that his father had promised that if he were with his father, he would be sent to college. It was, of course, unusual for a ten-year-old to be so concerned about college, and the court refused to consider this preference of the child which obviously had been induced by the enticement of the father.

In cases where one parent has succeeded in instilling in the child a particularly strong negative feeling for the other parent, the court is then forced, reluctantly, to give controlling weight to the preference. When the child is adamant concerning his choice and refuses to be with one parent, there is little in practical terms the court can do but honor that preference.

Such a situation existed in Rossi vs. Rossi,[8] where the trial judge conferred with the children, ages fifteen and ten, for an hour in private. The children exhibited extreme hatred and contempt for their father and absolutely refused to see or to be seen by him. The trial judge stated:

> I was able to perceive that the mother had been exercising an adverse influence over the children because it is quite unnatural that children of fifteen and ten years of age should exhibit toward their father the hatred that those two boys seemed to bear toward theirs. Under these circumstances, I do not see how the court could reasonably grant the father's petition.

From this, it would appear that the child's preference is a very real and difficult concept for the trial judge to resolve. Although a private interview by the judge with the child from a therapeutic point of view seems useful, it raises a number of legal questions regarding due process. *In camera* examinations of the objects of custody disputes have thus been attacked on the basis that the rights of no person can be determined by evidence procured by a judge through his own secret and private inquiries. The procedure for determining the child's wishes, as well as their admissibility and weight in trial, are matters of a broad discretionary power held by the trial judge.

Barbara Chisholm raises some very good questions in her seminal article on judges interviewing children.[9] "What protects judges from themselves and their own reactions, if the child's behavior, appearance, language, attitude and general demeanor offend or distress them? What assistance do they have with an unco-operative child who sits looking sullen or frightened and refusing to talk? How do they interpret such behavior as an aid to decision? Does the child's behavior reflect a perception of the judge as a person in authority? Or the child's feelings about the parent with whom the child is presently living, or unexpressed anger toward the absent parent? How should that influence the decision?

"And on the other side of the coin, does the child who is all too ready to talk, who smiles quickly and seems 'happy' and forthcoming, really provide the information that is needed? Sparkling children in a tense and unhappy situation are a contradiction of sorts. This behavior should ring a warning bell: the 'bright' behavior may be masking a depression far more serious than that revealed in the unpleasant behavior cited first. It is not easy to know the difference."

It seems obvious that the judge does not have all the skills required to make such an assessment in a single interview with a child. Most judges do not have training in child behavior and interviewing techniques. This is not to suggest that judges are not well-meaning, but rather to point out the difficult, if not impossible task they are given.

Child preference, as currently practiced, appears to have many shortcomings. However, it is one of many methods used to help litigate custody disputes.

Another method of trying to litigate custody disputes is the use of a separate legal representative for the child or children.

Numerous articles and judicial decisions have raised concern for the rights of children. During the International Year of the Child (1979) many bodies explored various methods of protecting the rights of children during divorce. The appointment of a lawyer, or advocate for the child, was one of several recommendations.

Legal representation for the child is usually urged on the basis that a child may have his or her own interests and that those interests may conflict with either parent during a custody battle. In other words, in a court proceeding regarding custody, the child's interests may not necessarily concur with those of one or the other parent. For example, one parent might decide that it is in his or her best interest (legally) to prolong a settlement in order to gain an advantage. The child's interest, on the other hand, is best served by a speedy settlement so as to end the psychological trauma and preserve a sense of security. A long and embittered court dispute may also jeopardize the child's relationship with one or both parents as well as with family members and close friends. In a protracted custody suit, the child may become the pawn in the parents' battle.

A lawyer who represents a parent in a custody case cannot really be thought of as representing what is in the best interest of the child. Nor is it reasonable to assume that the other parent's lawyer is going to represent the child either. Both are concerned with winning the case for his client. Indeed, one could argue that *if* the parents' lawyers were to represent the child in a custody dispute it would be tantamount to a conflict of interest.

Supporters of legal representation for children believe that the best interests of a child can only be determined on the basis of objective, independent evidence which shows what those interests are. This, according to advocates of legal representation, would get around the difficulty of having to deal with subjective opinion when deciding what the best interests of the child are. It is believed that a child who does not have legal representation will not have his or her views properly or completely articulated and presented to the court. Proponents of legal representation for children further argue that without legal representation a child may be at the mercy of the parents' legal bargaining points.

There seems to be agreement, not only among some members of the legal profession, but also among those who work in the field of child welfare (psychiatrists, psychologists, social workers, and others) that in cases of child custody suits, the child must be protected from becoming a victim of a system that can lead to potential abuse of the child. In an article entitled "Divorce by Fire," Wayne Clark expresses this view and the reasoning behind it:

"Many lawyers say that children should have separate representation when custody is disputed and in uncontested proceedings if the court thinks it necessary. At the moment they are invariably innocent victims . . . because lawyers cannot be expected to downgrade the interests of their clients in order to advance the sometimes conflicting interests of the children."[10]

It would be difficult to find anyone who did not agree that children have rights to emotional security or to education–why then are they denied the right to a fair and just custody decision? The child must be considered as a *person*, not a piece of parental property or a cherished creature. A child is someone who should be afforded the same rights as any other human being.

Law professors Henry Foster and Doris Freed put the argument in clear terms: "This matter of independent representation by counsel so that children have their own lawyer when their disposition for welfare is at stake, is the most significant and practical reform that can be made in the area of children in the law. Given our predilection for the adversary format and the small likelihood that it will be abandoned in the foreseeable future . . . it is clear that reform should be directed at making the process functional, and to permit all interested parties . . . including children . . . to have independent counsel.

". . . children have individual interest apart from and sometimes in conflict with parental interests and those of society. Their interests are entitled to be heard, and under the established system the only way that it can be done is through independent representation. Counsel for either parent owes a paramount duty to his client and cannot and should not be relied upon to promote the interests of children unless they coincide with those of his client. . . .

". . . The child should have his day in court."[11]

If it is agreed and there seems to be enough evidence to support these views, then, how best is a child represented in a custody dispute?

There is no doubt that making a decision regarding child custody is an agonizing process for a trial judge because of the indeterminate standards and the heavy value-laden material that has to be considered before arriving at a final decision. Judge Harold Missal of the Connecticut Superior Court describes the process in a sensitive and personal way:

"The custody matters are the types that I get personally involved in, and when I go home I do lose sleep over them. I worry about whether I have done the right thing or the wrong thing or done what is best for the child. Now, I have had some serious criminal cases where some sentences were given to these defendants and then I felt I was doing my duty, period, and that is all there was to it. But with these custody cases, I take them home with me and I worry about them."[12]

The question posed above leads to other questions–under what conditions would a lawyer representing a child make the judge's decision less painful and less discretionary than it currently is?

First, we must see how in fact a child retains legal counsel. We must ask these questions: Does the child run the risk of getting caught in a game of consumerism? How does the child know when and which lawyer he is to retain? Assuming that these matters are clarified, how then does a child instruct his lawyer? Does the child have the ability or capacity to communicate what is in his or her best interest? Is his preference based on needs? On wishes? Or, is preference based on influencing strategies by either parent?

Still further problems arise when we explore the role that the lawyer plays in representing the child. An article by Kim Landsman and Martha Minow in the prestigious Yale Law Journal discusses research undertaken to try and describe that role.[13] Basically they were able to define two positions that lawyers represented, one being that of *advocate* and the other *fact-finder*.

The lawyer who sees himself as the child's advocate, represents the child in the same way as an adult client. The child's wishes direct the lawyer to act as a zealot in his role as advocate. The main issue for this lawyer is that he will be guided by the child's wishes and will not interpret what is in his best interests, as this would, in his view, defeat the purpose of the child having his own representation. The procedures he would take as an advocate would have him call and cross-examine witnesses, argue motions, and perform other tasks of a traditional trial advocate. Accordingly, "without full advocacy of the preference there would be little reason to have a child's representative at all."

The *fact-finder* role relies more on the stated powers of the court. This lawyer would be working to protect the child's interests rather than wishes in the pending court hearing. His principal role is that of an impartial investigator; his principal task is to ensure that all considerations regarding the best interests of the child will have been brought to the Court's attention. Rather than advocate a particular placement decision, the fact-finder submits a report to the judge; he does not necessarily participate in the trial.

The Yale study revealed a blurring of the two roles of advocate and fact-finder. In an interview with one of the lawyers who identified himself as an advocate, the lawyer stated that "One ought never to recommend something contrary to the expressed wishes of a client." The study goes on to say, "He followed this philosophy even with a 13-year-old client who failed to provide what he considered 'terribly good reasons' for wishing to avoid visitation with the non-custodial parent. The attorney cross-examined witnesses at the hearing, arranged for and attended an interview in chambers between the child and the judge, and submitted an argumentative report with a recommendation that supported the child's expressed wish."

The study further uncovered a number of discrepancies between *what* the advocate stood for and *how* he functioned. The same attorney mentioned above, in spite of his philosophy, describes a case situation where he promoted the opposite view of the child's expressed wishes. In this case the child wished not to visit the non-custodial parent and told the lawyer that he wouldn't do so even if he were forced to. The lawyer, when recommending that the child visit his father, gave the following reasons: "It is probably the first case in which I have represented a child that I took a position contrary to his expressed wishes. I could not have done that conscientiously had I not had the input from a social worker (who had been working with the family for some time) that the child really did want to see his father and just didn't want to be responsible for making that decision."

In summary, the advocate was able to describe his role clearly at a theoretical level, but in the actual carrying out of his task there seemed to be a broader role where many more tasks were undertaken in trying to help the child and the family see what was in their best interests. The lawyer did not strictly adhere to his theoretical position of presenting and advocating the child's wishes.

The lawyer who identified with the role of fact-finder, functioned for the most part as an investigator. He tried to shed as much light on the situation as was possible. In essence, those who functioned as fact-finders also deviated from the strict investigatory role. In many instances they, like their advocate counterparts, tried to bring about an out-of-court settlement by using negotiation and mediation. One of the main criticisms that emerged from the Yale Study was that the "short-coming of the theoretical conceptions of the role of attorney for the child is their failure to recognize the importance of mediation, negotiation, and settlement, which persistently appeared in attorney interviews."

The point is made a number of times throughout the study that either view–the lawyer as adversarial advocate, or the lawyer as fact-finder–does not function properly for the child because the child is perceived as a person whose interests, once determined, must by law prevail. "This [the attitude expressed above] undermines the adversarial assumptions of the advocate role, because legal representative for the child's interest may as properly seek to mitigate the adversary nature of the conflict as to participate in it." In other words, the research suggests that a great deal of the work performed by lawyers is in the realm of dispute resolution using the very methods that divorce mediation advocates. It is paradoxical that lawyers who are hired to represent children find themselves going beyond the role of lawyering and for the most part find themselves functioning as mediators. They meet at times with parents, the parents' lawyers, the children themselves and all others who are relevant to the dispute.

One important difference between a lawyer and a mediator is that the mediator is highly skilled in the art of negotiation and dispute resolution, whereas the lawyer's training is in the realm of advocacy and investigation. In other words, the lawyer is trained in the art of advocacy, having reasoned argument as his forte, whereas the mediator is trained in the art of freeing people to make their own decisions.

In a recent child welfare case[14] the judge was asked by the mother's counsel to clarify the function of the child's lawyer. In her clearly reasoned response, Family Court Judge Rosalie S. Abella stated the following:

"I am persuaded that essentially the role of the lawyer for the child is no different from the role of the lawyer for any other party: He or she is there to represent a client by protecting the client's interests and carrying out the client's instructions. At the same time, the lawyer is an officer of the court and as such is obliged to represent these interests in accordance with well-defined standards of professional integrity.

"There is a tendency to assume that the quintessential legal representative for the child is, or should be, a paragon of legal, psychological, and sociological expertise. This is unrealistic. Lawyers generally have only legal skills, the proper utilization of which may undoubtedly involve some direct or indirect familiarity with or reliance upon other disciplines. Lawyers are called upon, in short, to exercise informed legal judgment. Lawyers for children can therefore be expected to do no more and no less than any other party's lawyer in the adversarial process. This is not to endorse the adversarial process in matters of family disputes. It is rather to acknowledge that it is through this process at present that these disputes are resolved. So long as the forum is the courtroom, the child's lawyer should represent his or her young client in a way which reflects equal participation with the other parties in this forum.

"Representing a client in these cases usually involves executing a client's instructions and, without being misleading, attempting to show through the evidence that these instructions or wishes best match the child's needs. In other words, a mother who wishes custody of her child expects her lawyer to present her case in such a way that her wishes are shown to be in the best interests of the child. It is, in most cases, an articulation of the client's subjective assessment, rather than the lawyer's. It should be no different when the client is a child. Where, therefore, the child has expressed definite views, these views, rather than those of the child's lawyer, should determine what is conveyed to the court. The child's advocate is the legal architect who constructs a case based on the client's views.

"In its purest form, that means that the child's lawyer should present and implement a client's instructions to the best of his or her ability. And this, in turn, involves indicating to the court the child's concerns, wishes and opinions. It involves, further, presenting to the court accurate and complete evidence which is consistent with the child's position. And too, there is an obligation to ensure, insofar as this is possible given the age and circumstances of the child, that the opinions and wishes expressed by the child are freely given and without duress from any other party or person.

"In child welfare proceedings, the court is obliged at the disposition stage to make an order 'in the best interests of the child.' This is defined as, among other things, 'the views and preferences of the child, where such views and preferences can reasonably be ascertained.' In other words, they are the views and wishes of the child, not those of his or her lawyer which should guide the court in attempting to achieve a resolution which most closely coincides with the best interests of the child.

"In many cases it is almost impossible to unerringly assess what is best for a child. Given this epistemological gap, why should the lawyer substitute his or her own opinion for that of the child. Consider too that a lawyer who formulates an opinion of the child's best interests is often making this judgment before the trial and therefore without the benefit of hearing all of the available evidence. Not even the most Solomonic of judges would be expected to perform this feat.

"In a trial it is for a judge to determine ultimately what is in a given child's best interests. The bases for this determination include, among other evidence, the child's wishes. These wishes should therefore, whenever possible, be articulated so that the court has the benefit of knowing of all relevant factors and so that the child has an effective and meaningful role in the proceedings which affect him or her no less than any of the other parties.

"There must undoubtedly be a degree of flexibility in a child's lawyer's role as articulator of his or her client's wishes. The child may be unable to instruct counsel. Or the child may be, as in this case, ambivalent about her wishes. Or the child may be too young. Although there should be no minimum age below which a child's wishes should be ignored–so long as the child is old enough to express them, they should be considered–I feel that where a child does not or cannot express wishes, the role of the child's lawyer should be to protect the client/child's interests. In the absence of clear instructions, protecting the client's interests can clearly involve presenting the lawyer's perception of what would best protect the child's interests. In this latter role of promulgating the infant client's best interests, the lawyer would attempt to guarantee that all the evidence the court needs to make a disposition which accommodates the child's best interests is before the court, is complete, and is accurate. There could in this kind of role be no inconsistency between what is perceived by the lawyer to be the child's best interests and the child's instructions. Where there is such conflict, the wishes of the child should prevail in guiding the lawyer.

"In the case of a child who is capable of coherent expression, the lawyer's role in representing the child's wishes does not preclude the lawyer from exploring with the child the merits or realities of the case, evaluating the practicalities of the child's position and even offering, where appropriate, suggestions about possible reasonable resolutions to the case. Offering advice is part of the lawyer's obligation to protect the client's interests. Obviously, however, given the vulnerability of most children to authority in general and given the shattered sensibilities in family disputes in particular, great sensitivity should be exercised during these exploratory sessions. The lawyer should be constantly conscious of his or her posture being an honest but not an overwhelming one.

"This case involves a 7-year-old girl who expresses ambivalence about where she wants to live. She has offered no clear instructions to her lawyer. Counsel's role in protecting her client's interests would include, therefore, articulating, exploring and attempting to explain this conflict to the court by evidentiary means. Then, having heard the evidence of all parties, the child's lawyer could further assist the court by offering in final submissions her assessment of what the evidence reveals to be in her client's 'best' interests."

It seems sensible to enhance the lawyer's role as a child representative by making it mandatory that lawyers entering the specialized field of child representation be trained in the art of mediation. This is, in fact, now being tried in a number of jurisdictions as well as in some law school curricula. There is no doubt that children need legal representation, but they need a lawyer with special skills. Such lawyers, at this time, are not readily available. The current trend of equipping lawyers to take on the specialized function of mediation is a significant advance in the difficult area of child custody.

The value of using mediation techniques is perhaps the main reason for judges to use pre-trial conferences which is another form of mediation which capitalizes on the inherent authority of the judiciary. The concept represents an even greater development in the integration of law and the social sciences as the judge himself is placed in the role of mediator, attempting to facilitate dispute resolution before the case moves on to trial.

Justice A. Leiff, in his article on the pre-trial conference comments on the importance of the conference as a forum for both counsel and client.[15] Lawyers can step out of their professional adversary roles and become active participants in sorting out facts and issues, of which they may have been unaware previous to the conference. "In a substantial number of cases, the pre-trial conference eliminates the defended trial and in any event, a better trial is achieved." The pre-trial conference offers litigants an opportunity to settle differences and dispose of issues without further litigation. This reduces delay of proceedings as well as expense.

I would recommend, as the Yale law researchers did, the following principles as a guide in the important area of child representation:[16]

1. The attorney should invite the child to participate and should provide explanation to the extent of the child's desire and capacity. He should also respect a child's desire not to participate. Although meeting with a preschool child is rarely worthwhile, the perceptiveness and ability to comprehend of even young school-aged children should not be underestimated;

2. The attorney should be wary of opposing the child's preference; there may be good reasons for the preference that are not obvious;

3. The attorney should act to enhance existing parent-child relationships; this requires a duty to the parents greater than avoiding the infliction of needless harm;

4. The attorney should take advantage of his unique opportunity to act as mediator and arbitrator in a manner consistent with the child's interests;

5. The attorney should exercise his own independent judgment and not simply rely on investigative agencies or experts;

6. Except with a preschool or disturbed child, professional evaluation of the child should not be sought where the child and his confidants can guide the attorney. This avoids needless introduction of strangers;

7. Where a psychological evaluation is necessary, the attorney should choose the expert and carefully instruct

him to provide information, not just conclusions. Professionals, moreover, should be used to help the child and his family, not merely to evaluate them;

8. If the attorney cannot settle the case and if delay will not serve his own trial strategy, he should press to have the case heard quickly and should play an active role in court.

The one recommendation that seems missing from this list of points is that lawyers must know how to work with an interdisciplinary approach so that professionals are not used as expert witnesses, but rather as a team whose function would be to bring their non-legal perspectives to bear on the situation. In short, "experts" should not be placed in the position of advocating the view of one client. They should instead be used to shed light on the case.

Chapter Nine

THE LAWYER'S ROLE

A major difficulty of family law is that the problems brought by clients are frequently not primarily legal problems; they are deep human problems in which law is involved. While the legal problems must be resolved, their resolution does not alleviate the human problem; and more importantly for the lawyer, frequently the legal problem cannot be properly handled unless the human problem is dealt with.

Family law litigation is unique among all legal actions in that it is almost invariably accompanied by the most intense and intimate emotions. It is rarely a cut and dried piece of business with a clear-cut beginning and end which can be handled and filed away. It is a painful process for all concerned–not the least of whom is the lawyer. When the psychological factors which affect the situation are not dealt with throughout the divorce process, the resulting complications come back to plague the lawyer again and again–bitter acrimony around child custody and visitation, non-payment of alimony and support, and so on. The list is all too familiar.[1]

Law Professor Gary Goodpaster, in trying to convince his legal colleagues as to the benefits of interviewing skills, states: "I am convinced, for example, that awareness and persuasion skills are at the heart of successful negotiations and trial advocacy. Negotiations and trials, therefore, must be studied not from the point of view of rules or formulas, but as persuasion events. Those who would train lawyers for such tasks must, to a certain extent, leave the law behind and become practical psychologists, with an intimate, real-world knowledge of how people influence one another and relate to one another in varying situations and contexts."[2]

Lawyers must know how to listen and how to persuade; in other words, how to deal with the emotional reactions of clients, opponents, and judges. We are talking about subtle awareness of the emotions and anxieties, and more importantly, mastery of the human interaction in lawyering–not for some pure motive such as concern for the human condition, but for very pragmatic reasons such as:

a) to find out the client's true feelings in order to save an enormous amount of wasted time and effort by recognizing and dealing with those clients who really do not want a divorce or custody of children despite all protestations to the contrary. This may represent revenge or be a face-saving ploy. A significant statistic–well known in practical terms to family law firms–is that one third of all divorce actions filed are withdrawn prior to court action. Clients are frequently too proud to approach a counselor with their problems or simply do not know where to turn but to a lawyer.

b) Another reason for the need to deal with emotions is to get the whole story so that there are no surprises at vital times in the legal process. Does this sometimes happen because the lawyer fails to get some essential fact from the client because he did not really listen, because he could not make the client appreciate the importance of every detail, or because he did not have good rapport with his client?

c) Awareness of the client's feelings helps prevent his undermining the legal process because of some unrecognized or unacknowledged emotions of his and helps the lawyer to anticipate realistically what is likely to happen in any given situation; and

d) to avoid the annoying cycle of the end of divorce proceedings marking the beginning of litigation around custody, access, and support.

In short, the lawyer needs to know how to recognize and deal with human emotions (or refer his client on to counselors if need be) in order to advance his own professional aims in each case.

A major difficulty of family law is that the problems brought by clients are frequently not primarily legal problems; they are deep human problems in which law is involved. While the legal problems must be resolved, their resolution does not alleviate the human problem; and more importantly for the lawyer, frequently the legal problem cannot be properly handled unless the human problem is dealt with.

What a lawyer may be unaware of or easily forget, sitting on his side of the desk, is that his role is invested with social power of great impact which puts him in an authority position which can (and usually does) intimidate the client to a greater or lesser extent depending on his position in the community and on his own sense of self. The lawyer is an authority figure, and the client–even if he is a professional himself with some power in the community–is in the powerless position of needing to rely on the lawyer's knowledge and skill for vital decision-making in his own life. In short, it is a reality that a vital part of the client's future will be determined by the outcome of this legal encounter.

Although most lawyers are not so impressed with their own power and may well be uncomfortable with both the fact of their own emotional impact on the client as a result of it and by the client's vulnerability at the crisis point in his life at which he approaches the lawyer–these are facts of life which must be dealt with. Emotions do not go away; they may go underground for awhile, but inevitably come back in unpredictable and frequently destructive ways, legally speaking.

Law schools do not prepare lawyers for the human arts of lawyering; on the contrary, the intense competition and rationalism of legal training may even work against a natural bent in this direction. Lawyers are trained to focus quickly and directly on acts and facts, not to deal with emotions. The psychological knowledge and specific behaviors underlying the effective exercise of the required skills have not been articulated for the legal profession.

A legal interview is a highly complex social behavior made up of a myriad of separate and interacting component behaviors. The following outline, though obviously an oversimplification, is a guideline. It should be noted that how successfully this guideline works will depend not only on the lawyer's skill in applying them, but on his or her personality.

Critical Aspects of the Initial Lawyer-Client Interview

I. **INTERVIEWING SKILLS**
   A. **Setting the scene**
      1. Greeting
         a. *Direct eye contact*
         b. *Calling the client by name*
      2. Indication of concern for physical comfort
      3. Indication of concern for emotional comfort, e.g. recognition that he had to wait for a long time.
   B. **Listening**
      1. Direct eye contact
      2. Complete attention, e.g. no telephone calls.
         a. *No extraneous movements, e.g. pen-tapping*
   C. **Communication: One cannot *not* communicate**
      1. Nonverbal clues: vital in both listening and responding
         a. *Postural, e.g. self-protecting: arms and legs crossed; leaning away. Holds for both lawyer and client, obviously both emotional beings. Important to be aware of personal responses, e.g. male responding to female, etc.*
         b. *Voluntary body movements, e.g. anger, pounding desk*
         c. *Involuntary body signs, e.g. flushing, sweating, coughing, stuttering.*
         d. *Facial expressions which seem inappropriate in relation to the words, e.g. smiling when talking about losing the children.*
      2. Verbal clues: Good indications of tension level
         a. *Tone of voice.*
         b. *Pace of speech.*

    c. *Use of pronouns such as "I," "You," "We." First-person pronouns put interview on a more equal basis. Effort to deal with authority barrier.*

    d. *Use of client's name. Interaction should be personal.*

    e. *Frequent use of affectively loaded (emotional) words by lawyer: gives client permission to express feelings. Also promotes feeling of closeness.*

II. **THE INTERVIEW:** The lawyer should not move too quickly into Problem-Solving. A problem can't be solved until it is thoroughly understood.

  A. The client should not be lead during his explanation of the problem, and the lawyer should stay out of his way until he finds out how the *client* sees the situation.

    1. The lawyer should provide limited structure through the use of an open comment or an invitation to talk, e.g. "Tell me a bit about your marriage."

      a. *Non-committal responses such as "I see" or "Mmm" or "Tell me about it" keep the flow of the client's thoughts and feelings going.*

    2. Use of questions

      a. *As neutral as possible and designed to help the client clarify problems for himself rather than specifically to provide the lawyer with information. This is difficult and may seem wasteful to the lawyer when he has required information to obtain, but going the circuitous route is often the shortest when dealing with the family law client. If he is lead where he is not ready to go, he will lose his train of thought and/or close off his real feelings. Result: The lawyer does not get the story as the client genuinely perceives it, the client's feelings often obscure and confuse his thought processes, and he undermines the legal plan.*

    3. Listening

      a. *The lawyer will note what the client says first. This is frequently an important clue to where he is emotionally.*

b. *Selective listening or listening through one's own perceptual field, that is, hearing only what you want to hear, should be guarded against. People tend to talk about what interests the listener. We unconsciously, through nonverbal body and attention clues, reinforce those subjects which interest us. Thus the client may be lead to where the lawyer thinks he ought to go before the whole story has been given on the emotional level.*

    i) Interpretive listening, which is not listening to gain an understanding of what is said, but to use part of what is said to further your own aims in a conversation, should similarly be avoided.

c. *Danger of using questions. Good interviewers and good cross-examiners know quite well that the form of a question tends to dictate the emotional reaction of the person interviewed and the form of the response to the question.*

    i) The person asking the question often has a pre-ordained answer in mind and puts words into the client's mouth; e.g. "Are you doing that because your husband pressured you?"

    ii) When asking questions, the lawyer should avoid "Why?" "How?" is better; e.g. "How did it happen that your husband did that?"

d. *The client should be given time to think about his answers to questions, without the lawyer jumping to conclusions.*

    i) A long silence may embarrass a lawyer, and can lead to his jumping in and putting words in the client's mouth which might not have been there. Many clients are too intimidated by the lawyer's authority to correct him.

e. *There are many ways not to respond while listening:*

    i) It makes sense to most people that responding to a client's story by warning him or by moralizing about what he should do makes him feel misunderstood and put down.

    ii) But what few people realize is that praising him, reassuring, sympathizing, consoling, and supporting may have the same effect. Trying to make the client feel better, talking him out of his feelings, or denying the strength of his emotions, e.g. "You'll feel better tomorrow" or "Don't worry, things will work out" impede the development of trust.

iii) When being reassured, the client feels that the extent of his painful feelings is not recognized, and that the seriousness of his problem is not understood.

iv) It is very difficult to keep ourselves from supporting and reassuring because we as human beings respond emotionally to a person's pain and naturally want it to go away–not only so he'll feel better, but so that we will, too.

v) Support and reassurance are better expressed through willingness to listen, a realistic appraisal of the problem, and recognition of whatever strength the client has demonstrated.

vi) In general the story should be accepted without reinforcing it in such a way that at a later point the client would find it difficult to tell other aspects of the story. e.g. If a wife tells a story about how awful her cad of a husband is and the interviewer supports the fact that he's a rotter, it becomes increasingly difficult for her to admit that she loves him madly despite everything and is just furious at him because of the other woman. You might not know until the day before the divorce that she really doesn't want a divorce and will withdraw the petition. Even the most experienced interviewer is frequently caught up in the drama of the initial presentation and sometimes finds it hard to maintain sufficient neutrality to avoid what may become a distortion.

4. Active Listening: Learning to decode a message sent by a client

   a. *What often goes wrong in communication is that there is a misunderstanding on the part of the listener or receiver of the message (in this case the lawyer) about what the sender (the client) intends. This may well be due to faulty sending, but the reason doesn't matter. Usually neither the sender nor the receiver is aware that there is a difference between the message sent and the message received, and each is proceeding on a faulty assumption.*

   b. *Accuracy of one's decoding may be checked by feeding back to the client how he has been heard; not the* content *of what he says, but the* feelings *underlying it. The lawyer shouldn't feed back his own opinions, evaluations, or reassurance; only the client's feelings. In this way, not only is the client's message checked out, but he has also been given the chance to clarify his feelings for himself.*

   c. *Example:*

      Client: (*Very emotional*) "What do you think I should do–run away, get a divorce, or just give in and take it?"

      The lawyer should resist all impulses to reassure, support, and/or offer solutions. All this will come later in a more beneficial manner.

      Lawyer: (*Noting tears*) "You feel low about your chances to resolve this right now," or "You're all tied up emotionally about your marriage. It's really getting to you."

   d. *Results of Active Listening:*
      i) Conveys to the client that the lawyer is with him, really trying to understand how he feels;
      ii) Crystalizes the client's comments by making him look at what he's saying, thus giving direction to the interview without leading him;
      iii) Provides a check on the accuracy of the lawyer's perceptions.

5. Patterns should be noted throughout the interview
   a. *especially inconsistencies or polarities of feelings or facts. e.g. Wife who berates her husband, but softens visually at certain points in her description of him.*
   b) *Most people have mixed feelings towards important people and situations in their lives. Reflecting this to the client may be especially valuable to him. e.g. Even when a marriage has ended, there are most often some positive feelings left for the spouse, and the client frequently needs permission to express them.*
6. Summarizing
   a. *Helps the client put his thinking together.*
   b. *Checks whether the lawyer has distorted the client's meaning.*
   c. Now *the interview may move from exploration to action, problem-solving, and legal advice.*

The above techniques are set out to help the lawyer in his negotiations of disputes which, as we have seen, is a fundamental requirement in settling conflicts and avoiding unnecessary litigation.

Chapter Ten

SHARED PARENTING: CAN IT WORK?

On some weekend afternoon, go to any zoo, park, or movie theater in your area and you'll find them easily: the single "Disneyland parents" trying desperately to amuse and care for their children during the few short hours that custody decisions allow them. Drive through your neighborhood in winter and you'll see the children, bundled to the eyes, grasping a toy, standing on the stoop, and waiting for the father that can't come in. How painful for both parent and child when that inevitable moment comes: "Be a good kid, I'll see you next week; remember I love you."

The late Frederick G. Gans, Barrister, brought sharply into focus the emotional pain felt by the parent who, when divorcing, must move away from his/her children, in an article entitled "The Non-custodial Parent: A Personal View."[1]

"It is my feeling that the non-custodial parent receives too little attention in the ultimate resolution of matrimonial disputes. More often than not, the non-custodial parent is the father who leaves the matrimonial home parting, at the one level, with all of the material things that he has built up and which provide elements of security for him. These material elements, needless to say, can be replaced if he is in favorable financial circumstances, and even if he is not, he's able to reconcile himself or accommodate himself to his new material situation.

"More important, though, is the fact that the non-custodial parent is the one who leaves the matrimonial

154

home and his children. If he has been at all involved in the upbringing and welfare, and day-to-day running of the children's lives, his withdrawal from that portion of his existence can be, and usually is, a devastating blow. Leaving aside the practical problems of relocation for the moment, more important to the non-custodial parent is the loss of day-to-day contact with his kids. If you run through your life with your children, examples from which you can draw are manifold.

"Separation by a father from his kids involves a number of things. For example, the noise at breakfast and at dinner, the stream of questions as to how high is up and things of that nature, the apple juice crawling its sticky way across the kitchen floor, all of these things are terminated very quickly. These little elements that we as parents seem to take for granted when our children are with us, are suddenly taken away and the non-custodial parent is met with nothing but deafening silence in his apartment.

"But in addition, implicit in the loss of custody is the loss of the right to govern the day-to-day activities and destinies of the child; the right to share with the child the hundreds of experiences that comprise his daily existence. He misses the millions of little things such as the hugs and the kisses, the dirty faces and the scuffed knees and elbows, and the privilege of tucking the child into bed at night and receiving a mushy kiss on the snoot and a 'Goodnight Dad.'

"It is little comfort to say to a father that he has adequate and generous access to the children. It is not the same as a day-to-day association with his kids. Nothing, not even telephone access on a daily basis, can replace the actual rubbing of elbows and nose-to-nose dealings he used to encounter.

"These things in addition to hundreds of others provide the embers for which a custody battle or confrontation between the mother and the father can suddenly be fanned up. This dislocation, and these deprivations of the father can provide and often do provide the food for the hostility which builds up between the parents. In addition, if the child phones and complains about the treatment he is receiving from his mother (whether it is justified or not), the father's reaction is usually one of anger, and he often feels that he can do a much better job than the mother is doing. If the child complains that he is lacking a toy or some other luxury, the natural tendency on the part of the non-custodial parent is to buy it on access days. This is an insidious way of undermining the position of the custodial parent who has the day-to-day care of the child. However, it is a natural thing and natural response because the non-custodial parent, faced with only limited time with the child, wants to make that child as happy as he possibly can, so that the visits are memorable, easy-going and enjoyable for everyone.

"Compounding the problem is the situation where the custodial parent suddenly takes on a new partner. The position of the non-custodial parent as father (or mother) suddenly becomes threatened whether there is reason to feel threatened or not. Mere mention of the third party sometimes is enough to cause a flare up. It is, I would suspect, a natural response of any parent to react strongly to the interference by a third party in the lives of his own children. Whether it is on a day-to-day basis or on an occasional basis, the parent must feel threatened. This will, therefore, temper his association with the custodial parent and often create terrible argument and confrontations between the two of them. These therefore can have an effect on the lives and destinies of the children, especially if mother and father are not getting on together.

"There are practical problems of access that must be faced by the non-custodial parent as well. The natural environment of the child, wherever he lives, is that area which surrounds his house. It is here that he builds up his peer association, it is here that little girls play with their girlfriends, little boys play ball-hockey and baseball, and it is here that they want to stay. Imagine the feelings on the part of the non-custodial parent when he rolls up in the middle of what looks like an extremely exciting ball-hockey game and the child complains about the fact that he has to go with Dad. The child does not understand how the father is feeling, the father often understands how the child is feeling, but can't back off and say "Well, I'll come back in an hour." If he does, the child usually has something else going at the time. So the father takes a position and stands pat on the fact that the child must go with him and the access days start off on a rocky footing. It takes a parent with an awful lot of empathy to be able to overcome this initial problem.

"Once he has the children in the car, what the devil does he do with them? How many times can they visit the Science Centre, the Museum, or the Art Gallery? How many things can you do with your children within the boundaries of the city that do not necessitate a drive in an automobile for half an hour or forty-five minutes? Sitting in a car with a restless child is, as you know, no fun. How many things can you do in the city which do not require the expenditure of some money? I don't refer to peanuts and popcorn but refer to major expenditures. Even a family entrance fee to the Science Centre is now $3.50. On a limited budget, it puts a terrible dent in the father's pocket.

"While with the child, the father is often confronted with the usual child trick of playing both ends towards the middle. The child often confronts the father with a ruling made by mother to seek his opinion on it, and (most probably) a contrary opinion. The reason is obvious: the child is going to flash back to Mom and confront her with Dad's view. It is very difficult to avoid the temptation to render an opinion on what goes on inside of mother's house, when the opinion is sought by the child.

"These are but a few points which a lawyer should bring to mind when about to dismiss a father's concern over access as a matter of little importance."

On some weekend afternoon, go to any zoo, park, or movie theater in your area and you'll find them easily: the single "Disneyland parents" trying desperately to amuse and care for their children during the few short hours that custody decisions allow them. Drive through your neighborhood in winter and you'll see the children, bundled to the eyes, grasping a toy, standing on the stoop, and waiting for the father that can't come in. How painful for both parent and child when that inevitable moment comes: "Be a good kid, I'll see you next week; remember I love you."

Today, traditional parental roles are changing rapidly. Women are entering the work force in large numbers, while many men have taken an increasingly active role in parenting their children. What this means for divorced couples is that traditional custody arrangements are neither adequate nor beneficial for children or former spouses. For these reasons, the idea of shared parenting has emerged recently as a positive step that may alleviate some of the painful problems. Proper circumstances are necessary, though, and in my experience the availability of a trained mediator is extremely important to success.

Usually there are two clear responses to shared parenting.

The first but less common reaction is intense excitement over a new and possibly workable solution to a thorny issue. If the concept is accepted as a serious effort to provide the emotional stability that children need without cutting off one parent, then it can be highly creative and innovative. It should not, however, merely be seen as "trendy."

The second and far more prevalent attitude begins with a horrified expression and ends with a statement like, "That's impossible–how could parents tear their children apart like that?" Without question, divorce is traumatic for children as well as for spouses.

Every child has an emotional bond with both parents that should not be arbitrarily broken. Is it better in every case for one parent to move out and become merely a special visitor on specified weekends? Or is it possible in some cases for the divorced couple to realize that parents really are forever and the best way to express this belief is to eliminate emotional and financial inequality by totally sharing the responsibilities of parenting? I pose these questions frankly, because the children of divorce have sat in my office crying for their parents to stop fighting, hoping they will not have to lose mother *or* father. This is an office that has become a child drop zone during custody battles when one spouse does not want the other to know a home address. It is a place where the senseless and destructive violence of custody has become very real.

The attitudes behind shared parenting are ably summed up by a woman who is my client. She reported that she told her husband, "I really don't want any legal custody hassles with you during the divorce, and I know you don't, so why don't we just agree that I'll take the kids, and you can visit them every Sunday." The father answered, "There's no way I'm going to wander around in parks for a few hours on Sundays with my kids, so why don't I take them and you visit." She was shocked by the suggestion, so much so that she said, "That wouldn't be acceptable to me either. I understand what you're saying, but what's to be done about it?"

There are many divorcing couples today who feel exactly this way. Fathers are unwilling to retreat to an apartment where, to quote one man, "The silence I thought would be so welcome turned out to be the most oppressive experience of my life." Like many fathers, this man couldn't live without the accustomed confusion, minor crises, colds, scraped knees, and jelly stains of his kids. These are the fathers who are unwilling to be "stuck" in an artificial situation with their children on visitation days with nothing to do other than take them out and buy them things, listening to them pour out their lives, lives they are no longer participating in.

Mothers who cannot tolerate the idea of assuming a similar role are also often unable to re-establish their own personal lives, have other adult relationships that are not secret, or start a career while caring for the children. This is not to say that these parents are not involved with their children, on the contrary, but they are also people who cannot cope with the traditional roles of divorced parents. It used to go without saying that, "The kids are better off with their mother." As we know today, this is not always true.

Some of these parents are finding that the idea of shared parenting is not only possible but beneficial for the entire family. Shared parenting is hard work for everyone; it is difficult to establish and maintain, but it is an extremely positive way to ensure that children are not traumatized by losing one parent. Parents do not have to assume an unnatural role, and children are less likely to be put in a position where they are playing one parent off against the other.

The following is typical of a joint custody agreement, principal residence with one parent, in a legal separation.

Now Therefore This Agreement Witnesseth

that in consideration of the premises and covenants hereinafter expressed and contained, the husband and the wife do covenant, undertake and agree, the one with the other, as follows:

1.   The husband and the wife hereby agree to live separate and apart from each other and each shall be free from interference, molestation, authority and control, direct or indirect, of any kind by the other party; neither party shall interfere in any manner with the other; and each party shall be at liberty to act or do as he or she sees fit; and to conduct his or her own personal and social life as freely and fully as if he or she were sole and unmarried; and neither of them shall take or cause to be taken any proceedings against the other of them for any cause or matter whatsoever arising out of or in any way connected with their marriage; PROVIDED THAT nothing herein contained shall constitute a bar to any proceeding which may be taken by either the husband or the wife for dissolution of their marriage, or to enforce any of the terms of this Agreement.

2.   The husband and the wife shall have joint custody of their infant children, provided that the said children shall continue to reside and have their principal place of residence with their father at _____ , in the City of _____ , and will continue to have as full a communication and contact with their mother as is reasonably possible commensurate with the best interests of the children, which shall include her right to have the children stay with her at her own residence for such days, weekends, holidays, and other periods as are reasonably convenient to

the wife, the husband and the children and consistent with the children's best interests and education. In the unlikely event there shall be any disagreement between the spouses concerning these periods, they shall consist of every Tuesday and Thursday and every alternative Friday after school until 8:00 p.m., every other weekend from Saturday at 10:00 a.m. to Sunday at 8:00 p.m., and one-half of the summer and mid-term school vacations. In addition, the children shall be free to eat lunch with the wife whenever it is reasonably convenient to both the wife and the children.

3. If at any time in the future the parties hereto realize and agree that the needs of the children require a change or alteration in the arrangements with respect to the residing parent such changes or alterations as are necessary or advisable will and shall be made without in any way affecting the rights of the parties as hereinbefore and hereinafter set out in this Agreement.

4. The husband and wife agree and undertake that in all matters relating to the custody, maintenance, education and general well being of the children, the children's interests shall at all times be paramount, and the husband and wife agree and undertake that in all matters they shall place their own separate convenience and interests second to the convenience and interests of the children.

5. The husband and wife acknowledge that they both desire that their separation should cause no emotional harm to the children. They undertake with one another that they shall at all times do everything necessary to ensure that the lives of the children are disrupted as little as possible. The husband and wife shall conscientiously respect the rights of one another regarding the children. The husband and wife shall continue to instil in the children respect for both their parents and grandparents and neither the husband nor the wife shall by any act, omission or innuendo in any way tend or attempt to alienate the children from either parent. The children shall be taught to continue to love and respect their parents.

6. The children shall be free to visit their mother at any time they wish and shall be free to communicate with their mother by letter and telephone as often as they wish.

7. The husband and the wife shall have the right to communicate with the children by telephone and letter at all reasonable times, provided that such telephone communication shall not interfere with the private life of the wife or the husband.

8. The husband and the wife agree that there shall be full disclosure between them in all matters touching the welfare of the children, and they agree that they shall confer as often as necessary to consider any matter requiring discussion, any problem or difficulty, touching the welfare of the children.

At present, the legal system does not recognize joint custody on a broad scale. (This is the legal term for shared parenting. I find this term too abstract and consequently don't use it.) Still, several states have amended their laws to *allow* for such a procedure. Clinical literature tells us quite clearly that the "visiting parent syndrome" in most situations is not a positive solution for children whose parents are *both* capable of providing sufficient care for them. Shared parenting can offer a viable alternative.

Even though it is still uncommon, one may explore shared parenting through referrals from judges and lawyers. It is possible for the mediator to help a family evaluate the feasibility of shared parenting. If it does seem worthwhile in a particular case, he or she may then assist in setting out the details and regulations.

There are many preconceptions and difficulties to overcome before shared parenting can become a functioning process. The initial fear that children may be torn apart between two separate homes must be balanced against the trauma involved in an artificial visiting-parent situation. The idea that the different lifestyles of divorced parents might result in conflict and disorientation has to be faced. What if the rag doll or the bicycle is at one home and not at the other? What about the conflicting loyalties that may arise due to the different regulations enforced in different households? Can children cope with the varying expectations of their parents any more than they could within the nuclear family?

After assisting in several working shared parenting arrangements, my own response to these potential problems is that children are far more adaptable than we as adults are willing to believe. School-age children especially have to enter an alien environment every day–an environment that has different surroundings, demands, and rules than their own homes–and they do this without undue stress. It is likely that they can adapt quickly to a shared parenting arrangement as long as they are aware of its shape and as long as it is consistently supported by each parent. It is generally a mistake to believe that children will predictably be torn apart by such a situation–rather, they have a tendency to feel more secure than they would under other conditions. This grows out of their awareness that, although their parents no longer live together, each one is actively participating in their lives; a type of security that does not usually arise from dismal weekend visits.

Divorce is never the best atmosphere for healthy growth in children. Even so, two direct questions must be answered in the face of the reality of divorce: Is traditional custody the only way to deal with the "disposal" of children? Is shared parenting a feasible alternative? My answer to the first question would have to be another question: Are the courts the first and only avenue for divorce? To the second question, my response would definitely be in the affirmative, providing that the conditions outlined here are fulfilled.

Shared parenting is not for everyone, and its benefits are available only to those families who are willing to make a considerable effort. When it works, shared parenting does not require a child to make a stated or implied choice between mother or father. It creates a situation instead where both parents are kept, where the tale-telling and present-buying inherent in Sunday parenting are not nearly so prevalent, and where each parent is able to re-establish a viable personal life during the times when the children are living in the other household. The prerequisites are adaptability and understanding on the part of the children and commitment and respect for viewpoints on the part of the parents.

A shared arrangement can improve or deteriorate for a number of reasons, including a child's maturing understanding of his or her parents, remarriages, or altered living conditions. The mediator's primary responsibilities here are threefold: first, he must be able to find out whether it is acceptable to parents and children alike as the best method of caring for the children; second, he should assist in setting up reasonable and fair living arrangements; and third, he must be available as an adviser as the arrangement continues. As in all types of mediation or arbitration, the mediator should require that he or she be consulted before any major actions are taken, particularly those involving the adversarial system.

Shared parenting is not a panacea for all the damage done to children by divorce, nor does it obliterate the fact that many divorced parents frankly dislike each other. Under the proper circumstances, though, the mediator will be present to act as a buffer between them. One of the major principles of mediation of any kind is to keep the welfare of the children foremost, and his or her role in shared parenting is no different. One caution should be paramount for anyone considering the idea: shared parenting usually requires more contact and co-operation between the spouses and it cannot be entered into as a means of maintaining an emotional bridge from wife to husband or husband to wife. This is no better than a custody battle, usually does not work, and often undermines the entire situation. A firm commitment from both spouses is necessary; mere acquiescence on the part of one spouse will not do.

Mr. and Mrs. Watkins were originally referred to me by their lawyers for mediation in the custody and access of their seven-year-old daughter Margaret. On the basis of several meetings with them, it seemed appropriate to explore the idea of shared parenting. Both seemed mature, rational, and fully aware that their marriage was finished. The sharing concept was eagerly accepted by each spouse, and an arrangement was worked out whereby Margaret would live with her mother for one week, her father for one week, and vacations would be split equally. The child's school would remain the same, both because she was doing well there and it was halfway, more or less, between the spouses' residences. Likewise, the costs of the child's maintenance would also be shared equally; this was possible in this case since both spouses had well-established careers. As the agreement was written, it was required that the parents would stay in touch with me during the ensuing months.

After this mediated agreement had been functioning productively for about six months, Adele Watkins met a man with whom she fell in love. Within another few months, they decided to live together and, as I later found out, they were quite willing to continue with shared parenting. Her friend, Richard, did not feel he had the right or need to interfere. During the year that shared parenting was in force, the Watkins had more contact than they would have had ordinarily; it was becoming a friendly interchange based on Margaret's welfare and the logistics of the situation. Before telling her former spouse about her plans with Richard, Mrs. Watkins foresaw that he would have to be reassured concerning respective roles, but she hoped that eventually he would feel secure about Margaret and happy for her in a new adult relationship.

Gordon Watkins' reaction was anything but predictable: "Oh, that's too bad, I was just going to approach you for a reconciliation. We seem to be getting along so well lately that I thought we were drawing back together." This put the mother in a real state of shock, for she had been convinced, as I was, that Gordon was finished with the marriage.

Needless to say, Mrs. Watkins' commitment to, and confidence in, shared parenting was badly shaken. She began to be concerned that the only reason her former husband agreed to sharing in the first place was to stay involved with her. Her suspicions seemed justified when Margaret began to ask why mother and father couldn't live together again. The situation was deteriorating rapidly, and the only recourse was to interview everyone concerned to determine whether the arrangement could continue and whether Margaret's interests were being served. Gordon admitted that although he hadn't been completely aware of it at first, he was using shared parenting as a secret avenue for reconciliation. The knowledge that his former wife was committed to another relationship began expressing itself in plans to try for sole custody. Not only was he terrified that another man would replace him as a father, but he was also terribly jealous and bitter.

In this particular case, it was possible to determine several things: except for relatively minor recent incidents, Margaret was secure within shared parenting, gradually accepting that she was loved and cared for in both households. Adele felt that the situation was positive for her daughter, and Richard was not interested in replacing the child's natural father, although he did care for her. But shared parenting cannot exist as a wedge. Despite joint meetings among the former spouses and the boyfriend, no solution could be found where Gordon did not feel threatened. As he told me, "I know everyone is trying hard, but something's got to change in me before I'll be able to let Adele go completely and devote myself to Margaret."

The case of the Watkins family is still continuing. Through mediation, Adele and Richard agreed not to move in together for a period of three months. For his part, Gordon promised not to enter into any legal proceedings for the same period of time. This compromise was reached so that Gordon might have some time to accept the idea that the marriage is over but not the parenting. In the meantime, Margaret is staying with her mother at Gordon's request.

Shared parenting only works when both parents are completely committed to it. If it is to work at all in this instance, Gordon must be able to accept it for what it is. This case illustrates that there are risks in shared parenting and that a great deal of certainty is necessary before it will be workable. Not only that, but considerable attention is required to keep it functioning properly.

In my experience, this is an unusual case; people who are willing to entertain the idea of shared parenting are generally able to recognize the pitfalls beforehand. As has been mentioned, however, the concept is not a cure-all.

A more usual and positive picture of shared parenting may be seen in the case of the Henderson family. Peter and Joanne Henderson were married in the sixties, they produced one son, Mike, now eleven, and one daughter, Kate, now ten. The Hendersons separated in the mid-seventies and were legally divorced in 1977. During their separation, the children both lived with their mother and the father was allowed generous access. As time progressed, it became apparent that Kate preferred to live with her mother, while Mike was closer to his father. This was not the result of jockeying on the part of either spouse, but simply emotional attachments that seem fairly predictable in such a family. Joanne suggested that they split the children between them to allow for their preferences, but Peter did not want to lose either of his children, even though he might be gaining one.

Through conversations with his friends and reading, Peter became aware of shared parenting. Not knowing quite how to set this up himself or how to approach his former spouse, with whom he did not communicate well, he was eventually put in touch with me by a mutual friend. After meeting with both people, it became clear to me that this couple was not at all interested in reconciliation, yet each one was very much involved in the welfare of the children. A series of brief interviews resulted in a sharing agreement stipulating that both children would live with each parent during alternate weeks. Joanne and Peter arranged to live within three blocks of one another so that schools and neighborhoods would continue constant and undue disruption would be prevented.

This situation has been working well now for eight months.

For the details, it is probably better for the Hendersons to speak for themselves. (Their identities have been disguised, but it might be interesting to know that the family agreed to be interviewed on tape specifically for the purpose of this book, because they all believe that shared parenting should become better known.)

Peter: "I really can't believe that this is working so well. Joanne's been just great about it. We worked out the details at her house. The kids knew that it was my idea and I think they were afraid this might cause problems. But it was Joanne who made up the calendars with different colors representing the alternate weeks, so we'd both have something to put on our fridge. The kids accepted the fact that we both wanted to do this and it quieted many of their fears about it."

Joanne: "Well, we told them [the children] that we were trying something new; that we were kind of pioneers, and we'd all have to work hard to make it go well. This intrigued them and they began to get excited about it."

Peter: "Of course, we were concerned about the kids getting disoriented, but since our places are so close together there really doesn't seem to be any problem. The first few times the switch was made there were a few problems about homework, but these have been cleared up. It was just that at the time there were too many things going on in their lives."

During the interview, I asked several questions involving possessions and how rules were made. Joanne told me that many of Kate's things stayed at her house, but she had quite a few at Peter's and didn't seem to mind because she always knew where they were. Many of Mike's things, his bike and so on, were usually at his father's house, but Mike, too, didn't seem to mind this arrangement.

Mr. and Mrs. Henderson certainly do have conflicting philosophies and these are expressed to some extent in their lifestyles.

Peter: "I'm not as strict about cleaning up the house, but I am adamant about homework, making time to talk, and not watching so much television. There were a few times when one of the kids would say that they were allowed to watch this program or that at their mother's, but I explained that we felt differently about these things, and that this was how it was to be here. In thinking about it now, I'm amazed that they understood this and accepted it so quickly. Regulations are very important, you have to make it clear that the time spent with you is normal time, not playtime. The kids have to realize that you have your lifestyle and it has to be respected."

Joanne: "At first, I was very concerned that the kids would pick up bad habits outside. Peter's not the neatest person in the world, but it seemed to work out well once the kids understood that we lived different lives. While I'm trying to relax after a hard day, I sometimes don't have the energy to spend with them, and I admit that they were really getting hooked on television. This was mostly when I was caring for them myself, but now that they spend alternate weeks with Peter this has been cut down and I'm pleased about that. With some time off, I find I have more time to spend with the kids when they are with me. Because we live pretty close together, possessions really aren't a problem. We don't get into duplicating things, neither of us could afford it anyway. In some ways, it's good for the kids to have to plan what to bring from one place to another."

I spoke to the children, Mike and Kate, to find out what they thought about the situation. They told me that they really weren't too hopeful in the beginning, but "Mom and Dad wanted to try it." Now, they had nothing negative to say about the arrangement. Kate thought her father was tough about homework, and Mike didn't like having to keep his room at his mother's so clean, but these things were said more in a tone of grudging admiration than anything else. To the question whether they liked being able to know both their parents in this manner, rather than living with their mother and having their father visit as in the past, they both said it was a great idea.

This is working and is, in some ways, an ideal situation. The calendar is really quite fluid; if one spouse has a week off, then it is quite possible to rearrange schedules to suit conditions. Although Peter and Joanne do not communicate well, they are completely committed to the idea of both providing the affection their children need. In Joanne's words, "I would never give up my kids, but I can't expect Peter to either. His ideas are different than mine, but he's a good father. It wouldn't be fair to cut the kids off from that." Peter said quite simply, "Joanne and I don't get along, that's why we're divorced, but we can't let that get in the kids' way."

Although it was not a basic reason for entering into shared parenting, Joanne is finding that there are some adult-type benefits in the situation. "When the kids were both living with me all the time, I couldn't really go out much myself. There was always the problem of babysitters and I really didn't feel I could ask Peter if I was dating somebody. There were other problems. I mean, what if I met somebody that I wanted to be with? I really couldn't stay out late or anything, and it got to be quite difficult. Now, since the kids are away every other week, I can begin to have a social life and this is very good for me. I know they are getting the best care and I don't have to worry."

Peter's reaction is similar: "You know, when you're married you really don't get involved in some things with your kids. You know, little things like doctor's visits and dentist appointments. I remember the first time we went out to buy clothes. In the past, I had never done this with the kids, and it was really an incredible experience to watch them picking out things they liked. The same kind of thing happened when we went out to buy food. I didn't stock the kind of stuff they like at first, and they thought it was a riot that I didn't know what Fruit Loops were.

"Socially I guess my life has changed, too, it's more restricted now than it was, but I really don't mind. I feel much easier now about my whole life, knowing that I'm participating in my kids' lives. I can't tell you how bad those Sunday visits were. I kept thinking, 'Christ, what are we going to do now?'"

Joanne: "Peter and I have talked about what might happen if anything more permanent comes up in either of our lives. No decisions have been made about that yet, and I think we both hope we'll be able to work it out if it does. We did tell the kids that we were kind of pioneers in this, and I guess we are, so we'll just have to overcome that obstacle when it turns up."

To me the most encouraging thing about the Henderson family is that the children, Mike and Kate, find their lives quite normal. They feel secure in the knowledge that both parents actively love them. During my joint interview with them, I think they were beginning to wonder what was wrong with me, because I suppose I was looking for reactions and problems that just were not there.

Right now, this situation is functioning at a highly successful level, but it should be remembered that neither Peter nor Joanne has entered into any long term emotional relationships that might have a tendency to threaten one or the other in their parental roles. From observing the family closely, however, I would have to say that each of the inner family relationships is very strong. It would seem unlikely that emotional ties outside this unit would affect it negatively. The greatest single reason that shared parenting is working so well for them springs from the fact that neither spouse is emotionally involved with the other. On this basis, it would be extremely difficult to shake their commitment.

Shared parenting is a new movement in the resolution of the divorce struggle where the mediator can be particularly useful in helping clients break new ground. Such a solution to custody has a wide range of positive aspects, even beyond those already mentioned. It has a definite tendency to assuage the guilt that grows out of divorce, especially the guilt felt by the spouse who initiated divorce proceedings in the first place. The former visiting parent is relieved of a great deal of the financial burden of maintenance and amusing the children on visitation days. A sharing situation allows both parents equal free time as we have seen. In addition, it also tends to prevent the kind of resentment felt by the custodial parent that is usually expressed, "He's out having a ball, while I'm stuck here."

Both parents participate for extended periods in the developing lives of their children, and the children do not have to lose either one of them. While they are in the care of one spouse, all the responsibilities of that care fall on the individual parent. This includes such things as P.T.A. meetings, doctor's appointments, and so on. The extended nature of shared parenting also permits both sets of grandparents to have more time with their grandchildren. In law, they actually have no rights and, as discussed earlier, limited access to the grandchildren is most often a crushing blow to older people.

Shared parenting also has definite drawbacks and pitfalls. When emotional involvement is continuing on one side or the other, the arrangement is not only unworkable but damaging to everyone. One parent cannot simply agree to the idea to prevent further arguments; there must be a very strong commitment on both sides. It is quite possible, further, that one parent might have the best intentions, but may prove to be irresponsible in his or her own behavior. In such a case, sharing is not possible. One fact in any discussion of custody should not be overlooked: when the acrimony between the spouses continues to run very high for a long period of time, a child will often make a decision to deny access to one parent or the other. The decision is based on self-preservation and is frequently the only way out. Again, in such a case sharing is not feasible. There are also financial limitations, because sharing requires that each parent maintain a home that will accommodate the children and each has to shoulder equal financial responsibility. Nevertheless, the mediator is sometimes able to negotiate finances if, for instance, the mother is not able to afford complete parity with her former spouse.

When all the pluses and minuses of shared parenting are presented, a balance must be struck with the images of the bewildered Sunday parent and the forlorn child on the stoop. Custody decisions are handed down by judges who will freely admit that they cannot evaluate the situation fairly. Each parent presents a case, and the judge, like an unlucky Solomon, must determine which one is unsuited to care for the children on the basis of pleading, not fact. This is an incredibly difficult and frustrating situation for a judge to be in, and he knows that more often than not custody decisions come back to haunt the court again and again.

The winner of a custody suit is inevitably left with a large share of guilt for the victory. The loser, on the other hand, can only harbor anger and resentment. It is difficult to understand how the court's decision can be explained to children who have probably been exposed to the adversarial system to one degree or another. How can one tell a child that although Daddy or Mommy is unsuited to be a parent, he or she will be coming to visit? The damage done to children and the unresolved guilt or hostility created by these decisions is extremely destructive. Little wonder that shared parenting is becoming increasingly more common in those families who are aware of what happens in adversarial custody suits.

Despite the fact that it appears to be an eminently sane way of dealing with the question of custody, no significant research has been done on shared parenting. Mediators, family therapists, judges, and lawyers who have assisted in shared parenting have a definite responsibility to develop their research and report their findings to help guide the growing number of families who might be benefited by it. We are operating today from educated guesses and practiced wisdom when dealing with this new concept. This is not good enough. Empirical research must become the basis of clearly set out methods, so that shared parenting may continue to develop.

In a recent case, New York Supreme Court Judge Shea, describes in a clear and thoughtful way the issues on both sides of the question of shared parenting (joint custody).

Joint custody is an appealing concept. It permits the court to escape an agonizing choice, to keep from wounding the self-esteem of either parent and to avoid the appearance of discrimination between the sexes. Joint custody allows parents to have an equal voice in making decisions, and it recognizes the advantages of shared responsibility for raising the young. But serious questions remain to be answered. How does joint custody affect children? What are the factors to be considered and weighed? While the Court should not yield to the frivolous objections of one party, it must give thought to whether joint custody is feasible when one party is opposed and court intervention is needed to effectuate it. In the end, as in every child custody decision, it is the welfare of the children which governs and each case will turn on its individual facts and circumstances.

It is well recognized that the children of divorce are subjected to severe strain, and that children often experience loss of security and feelings of rejection as a concomitant of their parents' separation. Experts in the field have expressed opposition to divided custody on the ground that change and discontinuity threaten the child's emotional well being. It is argued that joint custody between parents usually requires that 'shuttling back and forth' of children which must inevitably lead to the lack of stability in home environment which children require. Moreover, joint or divided custody may exacerbate the adults' use of the children to defeat each other in defiance of the children's interest in stability, serenity and continuity. In attempting to maintain positive emotional ties to two hostile adults, children may become prey to severe and crippling loyalty conflicts.

The proponents of joint custody contend that fathers relegated to seeing their children only intermittently experience feelings of deep loss and often react by limiting their involvement with their children. They argue further that there is no scientific data for the *de facto* preference in favor of the mother and that fathers in today's dual career families are equally nuturant and competent to care for their offspring. They contend that a child needs a sustained involvement with both his parents and that the conventional single parent custody arrangement tends to make ex-parents of fathers, painfully deprived creatures out of the children, and overburdened people out of mothers.

These are persuasive arguments. No post-divorce custody arrangement will give to children two loving parents, living together, devoted to each other and to the children's welfare. Joint custody, under the proper circumstances, may be the closest it is possible to come to the shattered ideal. The courts, in dealing with the difficult issues raised by child custody litigation, should consider joint custody as an option, particularly in performing their little noted but frequently exercised role as mediator before trial.

However, when one parent resists joint custody and refuses to be persuaded that it is workable, what will be the result for the children when it is ordered by the Court? There appear to be no social science studies that will answer this question. The most ardent professional proponents of joint custody assume cooperation between parents and agreement about child rearing practices as basic requirements for joint custody. It is hardly surprising that joint custody is generally arrived at by consent.

It is understandable, therefore, that joint custody is encouraged primarily as a voluntary alternative for relatively stable, amicable parents behaving in a mature civilized fashion . . . As a court-ordered arrangement imposed upon already embattled and embittered parents, accusing one another of serious vices and wrongs, it can only enhance family chaos.[2]

The point is again stressed that joint custody or shared parenting may be a viable alternative only when certain conditions are met: when both parents are committed to the idea of shared parenting and can hold their children's best interest as paramount to their own needs; when the logistics as to where the parents and children reside, are so arranged that there is not a major problem regarding schooling, friends or other important social contacts; and finally, when the child can handle at a psychological level the kind of adjustments which are necessary when he is residing part of the time with one parent and part of the time with the other. Perhaps the overriding issue is that the parents must set aside the marital conflicts and not undermine each other in child rearing matters. It should be noted, however, that some conflicts are inevitable and may not be destructive.

This is an ideal situation for divorce mediation. Many couples in a shared parenting arrangement will agree on a mediator to help them when conflicts arise. This stops them, at least initially, from involving lawyers and courts to try and resolve their disputes. At first, parents may get into difficulty regarding what seem to be very minor issues, such as who is going to take the boys to religious school. "Why is it that Sally watches television at her father's when I have made a rule that she is not allowed to watch television on a school night?" "When Leo returns after the week with his mother, he tells me that I don't know how to cook and that his mother gives him good meals and I give him all this junk food."

There is no doubt that shared parenting cannot replace a traditional family situation that has love and harmony, although we must admit that many intact families have severe conflict when it comes to difficulties between the parents regarding child-rearing practices. The conflicts described above can be resolved through mediation and it is only when they are left unresolved and when lawyers and the courts start sending threats and warnings back and forth that the minor problems escalate into very serious family discord.

Many lawyers today will say that the use of a mediator in a shared parenting situation saves a great deal of time and energy normally spent listening to the complaints of their clients when unable to do much about them. It is in these cases that a lawyer will involve the mediator to try and help resolve the family dispute.

There is a recent study conducted by Dr. Judith Greif, chief social worker of the Division of Child Adolescent Psychiatry at the Albert Einstein College of Medicine. She reported that despite arguments that joint custody can only work in the absence of hostility between the parents, "Where there is a common concern for the child, that is enough to assure the arrangement will work."[3] I find this in my own practice too: when conflicts between parents do not lead to problems for the children, the situation remains viable. This view challenges the BBIC (Beyond The Best Interests of the Child) extreme that joint custody is unrealistic, whereby they suggest only one parent should be awarded custody, including the right to limit or cut off entirely the other parent's visiting. Obviously if one takes the *BBIC* view, then immediately the parents are put into the situation, regardless of their personal views which may be to have a shared parenting arrangement, to hire "tough lawyers" in preparation for the eventual bitter custody battle. There is no doubt that the courts cannot impose joint custody against the wishes of one parent. Even when the courts make a decision in favor of joint custody the conflict that was created during the custody battle is too deeply felt by everyone and the likelihood of the joint custody arrangement working is practically nil. What is needed is an opportunity for parents to discuss openly and honestly between themselves, the mediator and the children, when indicated, as to whether or not shared parenting can work for them. To try to impose this arrangement after bitter accusations seems at best looking for a solution to an insoluble problem.

Some further results of Greif's study revealed that "There is a different quality of psychological involvement that evolves from the opportunity to take care of (i.e. to parent) one's child, rather than visit with one's child." She further states, "You find that those things the custodial mother is complaining about having too much of–saying no, getting to bed, helping to do homework–those are the things the visiting father doesn't have and wants more of."

Although the research to date, meagre though it may be, is just beginning to support some form of shared parenting and the findings by no means are conclusive, there are some assumptions that can be stated with a degree of certainty. One way to be helpful in this area would be to list some of the wrongs of shared parenting. The following is what I call **"How to fail at shared parenting:"**

1. The courts impose an order of shared parenting where one parent is dead set against it.

2. The courts impose an order of shared parenting where the child is dead set against it.
3. The parents agree between themselves to a shared parenting arrangement because one parent's chief motivation is that this will lead to a reconciliation.
4. The parents agree to shared parenting because one parent feels intimidated and is fearful that financial support will be cut off.
5. The parents agree to shared parenting because one parent feels guilty at ending the marriage and wants to make it up to the other spouse.
6. The parents agree to shared parenting but their living arrangements, i.e. work hours, proximity of residences, make it impractical.
7. The parents agree to shared parenting because they are pressured by therapists, marriage counselors, mediators, parents and friends.

When we sift through the pros and cons of shared parenting, we are left with a conflicting array of propositions based on traditional views of the family. This is the same situation in relation to other myths regarding divorce–staying together for the sake of the children; it is a sign of personal weakness if one makes a decision to leave the marriage, and so on. There are no right or wrong answers in relation to these matters. What we do know is that families, if given the opportunity through mediation, will resolve matters of custody in a far better way than having courts impose a ruling which they cannot live with. The process itself makes it difficult for the families to accept the court's decision.

Chapter Eleven

SUMMING UP

When a marriage is over, it is not the time for retribution and revenge, but rather the occasion to strike out for a new life while providing for and protecting the children. For many couples, a non-adversarial process such as divorce mediation provides an effective means of achieving these ends.

As it is now practiced, adversarial divorce with all its stress on fault, retaliation, win and loss, has no positive benefits for the contestants. Such legal battles over interpersonal relationships do not provide a healthy or just atmosphere for divorcing couples and their children. Lawyers are expected to act beyond their capabilities, judges must make decisions on matters outside their training and the system itself is labeled "unjust." In its mildest form, adversarial divorce is a sham, in its most violent form it is both a societal and personal disaster. The single winner created often has an enormous burden of guilt to bear, while the loser, if he or she is left anything at all, carries a soul-breaking weight of resentment and anger. Between the spouses, there is at least one legally sanctioned victor, but for the children there are only legally sanctioned losers.

Divorce is a symptom of the deep-seated distress of our society as a whole, a condition whose causes are deeply imbedded in our collective social history. Divorcing couples are not at fault. They are not responsible for the general malaise of society. Rather, they are prominent and numerous victims. The casualty list, as we have seen, is considerably longer than the mere one million couples who will divorce this year. Three-quarters of these marriages have children and all have satellite figures.

In the majority of adversarial divorces there is a great deal of conflict, pain and loss for the entire family. The loss must be attributed to the antiquated and frequently bizarre way we go about ending a marriage in our society.

It seems that the only guiltless way to be divorced is to find fault, to lay blame, to transfer the guilt, as it were, and take retaliatory steps against a person who was once loved. Marriage involves psychological complexities and it is all too true that our legal marriage technicians are not suited for the role of dealing with inner family problems, chiefly because they are not trained to deal with them. Divorces go to court, courts are essentially designed to handle crime, but divorce is not a crime. It does not properly belong within a system geared to search out and find a perpetrator. More often than not, there is no fault to be found, no guilt to be assigned. Even in cases where guilt might be rightly assigned, what purpose does it serve? The excessive tension created by the adversary system is added to the severe emotional tensions of marriage breakdown. There is an alarming tendency to take divorce into the arena of self-perpetuating destructive conflict which is characterized by a tendency to expand and escalate. Two people who have mutually agreed to separate may even be required to tell lies about one another to "qualify" for a divorce. In the search for a guilty party or for "grounds" the conflict often becomes independent of its initiating causes and things said and done become paramount long after the real causes of the marriage breakdown have been forgotten. "The expansion of the conflict depends on the dimensions–the size and number of the immediate issues involved, the number of motives and participants implicated on each side of the issue, the size and number of the principles and precedents that are perceived to be at stake, the costs that the participants are willing to bear in relation to the conflict, the number of norms of moral conduct from which behavior toward the other side is exempted, and the intensity of negative attitudes toward the other side."[1]

This definition of expanding conflict comes not from a book on divorce, but a study of dispute resolution, particularly labor relations. The author, Morton Deutsch goes on to quote Coleman who expresses it as creating "Gresham's Law of Conflict" in which "the harmful and dangerous elements drive out those which would keep the conflict within bounds."[2] Herein lies the kernel of divorce mediation: divorce exists, conflict between spouses exists, but it is not necessary to drive this conflict into destructive and expensive channels. Solutions need not only be imposed by one side or the other by using superior force, deceptions, or cleverness.[3] The adversary system requires conflict, but conflict breeds only more conflict.

Divorce mediation deals only with constructive conflict *resolution*. No one wins in the adversary sense of the word when using divorce mediation. But, everyone benefits. The days when penance had to be done for marital breakdown should end. Separation and divorce create emotional trauma, without adding the scourge of drawn-out acrimonious legal battles.

Contested divorce is not likely to disappear, but rational dissolution is possible, and divorce mediation has in many cases resulted in rational dissolution.

Divorce mediation does not intend to dispense with the legal profession. On the contrary many lawyers and judges have been in the forefront regarding family law reform. Furthermore, many lawyers are extremely effective in helping couples resolve their disputes and in referring their clients to mediation. Generally speaking, lawyers do not specialize, or if they do it is in such areas as corporate, tax, estate or contract law. These technical fields can be thoroughly learned from books and research. Thus far, domestic or family law has been given less status by the legal profession either as a legitimate course in law schools or as a legitimate speciality in practice. Recently, though, experiments have been attempted to teach law students basic interviewing and counseling skills. In my own experience, these include interdisciplinary classes where psychology, psychiatry, social work and law students react to a series of situations from within their own disciplines. The nature of such classes makes it possible for each discipline to gain considerable insight into the other. What, for example, does a psychologist know of law? What does a lawyer know of psychology? In today's world of specialist terminology they even speak almost separate languages.

There is an urgent need for family law specialists in North America. The only way that such specialists will be created is if our educational system is adapted to fill the need. Such lawyers would be equipped to determine whether a divorcing couple could benefit from a whole range of available expertise whether in the form of therapy, psychiatry, mediation, or arbitration. In many cases, it is for them to make referrals to qualified personnel who will be able to assist the family, just as it is for us to take advantage of what exists at the present time and to demand that this training be undertaken.

As many judges already know, it is necessary for the courts as a whole to understand the benefits of such an interdisciplinary approach to family disputes. It is all too true that many couples are not aware of the existence of court-based conciliation programs.

Divorce mediation also has advantages to the legal profession. One familiar statistic states that one third of all divorce actions filed are withdrawn prior to court action. By referring his client to a conciliation counselor early in the divorce proceedings, the lawyer may save himself an enormous amount of wasted time and effort in dealing with those clients who decide to reconcile and would have dropped litigation further along in the process. It is not uncommon for a client to approach a divorce lawyer knowing full well that he has no intention of going through with it. Such clients use the threat of divorce to control the spouse's behavior. Obviously if such clients are not helped to examine their behavior, the lawyer may well be involved repeatedly (and with a high annoyance factor) in an area where it is inappropriate for him to take part.

Given the high rate of divorce today, it seems quite reasonable to expect that most marriages, whether they continue or not, are occasionally troubled by thoughts of breaking up. It is time that the fear engendered by adversarial divorce be eliminated. It is time that if decisions are made to break up or stay together, they should be for the right reasons. Those reasons include the health, safety, growth and happiness of family members.

Even in its most friendly guise divorce is a destructive situation. Problems of split loyalty, guilt and loss are inevitable for the children. But if divorcing couples, therapists and the courts understand and build upon the procedures of conciliation and use divorce mediation, the lash of the courtroom will become unnecessary. When a marriage is over, it is not time to retaliate and take revenge. It is time to strike out for a new life while providing for and protecting the lives of children.

Whatever the accusations that are made in the course of seeking a separation or divorce, the basis of marital conflict goes beyond the stated. Most counseling approaches seek to dissipate inner stress. The idea is for people to learn to talk to one another rather than "act out" their emotions in a destructive way. The mediator aims to help couples identify issues and help them resolve their own disputes. The approach grows out of experience with the adversarial system. A dispute which is settled by court order leads to resentment and often, the couple is back in court trying to change the decision. A dispute which is settled by mutual agreement is more likely to stay settled. There is less resentment because the involved parties made their own decision with the help of the third party. The benefits to the children and to the family unit as a whole are real and tangible.

Some of the cause for this optimism is the result of research conducted at the Family Court in Toronto.[4] A demonstration and research project on conciliation counseling was carried out from 1976 through 1979 involving over four hundred families who participated in two research studies. Although still in preliminary stages, the initial results are most promising.

Approximately 70 percent of the families who were referred for conciliation reached an agreement without going to trial. The majority of these cases were custody and/or access disputes. Furthermore a follow-up interview some 3 to 4 months later revealed that 80 percent of those who had reached an agreement had either fully or partially maintained the original agreement. A second follow-up of the court records one year later, although not complete, appears to be holding the initial trend of 80 percent. Referrals from lawyers which are made earlier in the legal process seem to have a higher rate of agreement than those referred directly from the judge at the time of the hearing.

Another important finding is that the majority of cases reach agreement with fewer than six interviews. The model of brief or short term counseling seems to be most effective. The majority of the clients (70 percent) reported that things had changed for the better and that they had benefited substantially from the service.

In a related study, 53 lawyers were interviewed following their involvement with the conciliation service. Approximately 80 percent were in favor of the project and said they would recommend the service to other lawyers. The overwhelming majority of lawyers felt that the conciliation service was valuable in the following ways:

1. Helps avoid unnecessary litigation
2. Better prepares the parties to understand the issues
3. Allows the client to use legal services more appropriately
4. Reduces the clients' emotional turmoil.

Although many of the lawyers were not in favor of a mandatory conciliation interview the majority were in favor of a letter written by court which would urge the parties to use the conciliatory services prior to litigation. The Los Angeles Conciliatory Service in fact uses a similar procedure.

Empirical studies like the Toronto conciliation project are needed to validate the effectiveness of mediation services. The Family Courts in Edmonton, Alberta and Kingston, Ontario have also conducted research with similar positive results. The cost benefits of such programs to the public in both human and financial terms are now being substantiated through empirical research. In the United States, there will soon take place a "White House Conference on Families." During the early nineteen-eighties, submissions to the Conference will come from a great many organizations having to do with families, including the following recommendations from the Association of Family Conciliation Courts. (This is an international association of judges, counselors, behavioral scientists and lawyers, considered to be a leading association in the field.)

All families should have access to adequate family court services and family counseling services.
Legislation should be drafted to provide funds for local jurisdictions to establish family court services, including such functions as family conciliation services, custody evaluation services and domestic violence programs. A national institute for interdisciplinary training for judges, attorneys, and mental health professionals should be established. This legislation should also require development of a uniform statistical reporting system in the area of family law and domestic violence services, and would encourage the development of a "systems-approach" to reduce family fragmentation.
Medicare, medicaid, and private insurance companies should provide for reimbursement for family counseling by qualified vendors to insure availability and use of these services.

All persons prior to family formation and at critical life junctures should have access to training to prepare for these new roles.
Legislation should be drafted to provide for the development of relevant, preventive, educational programs at the time of family formation, in schools, and for parents to teach the roles of "spousing" and "parenting." This legislation would also provide for "well family clinics" and would encourage the further development of marriage and family enrichment programs to teach basic communications and conflict resolution skills. Also provided would be seminars for divorcing families, parent-effectiveness training for

families involved in the court system, and community awareness and sensitivity would be developed to family violence as a major problem needing solution.

Public and private programs should be co-ordinated to prevent family fragmentation.

Legislation should provide incentives for local agencies to co-ordinate and rationalize the service delivery system, including both private and public agencies where they impact the family. We also strongly recommend the establishment of a National Institute for Family Development to fund demonstration projects, subsidize interdisciplinary training, evaluate programs, monitor the effects of policy on families, and recommend legislation when appropriate. Under this legislation, we would recommend the treatment of problems through community based programs rather than through institutional means; regional clearing houses should be encouraged to further the co-ordination of services.

Economic, social and cultural stresses should be reduced to permit families to develop and flourish.

Legislation should be initiated to develop a nationwide system of child care centers for working mothers, which also would serve as stress centers for families when the caretaker needs "time out." Attached to these centers would be other resources that could relieve stress for families. An adequate national health program and full employment strategy should be provided for all families.

All family members should have the right to legal counsel.

Legislation should be created to mandate and fund the right of indigent fathers to be represented by counsel in child support cases through the same mechanism as is used to support the prosecution of these cases.[5]

As a member of the Board of Directors of the A.F.C.C., I lend enthusiastic support to these recommendations–perhaps the most far-reaching and realistic ideas to date.

From a practical perspective, the foregoing discussion brings into sharp relief two important issues to everyone involved in family litigation. The first issue concerns the availability of some alternative to the judicial process for couples in distress. At the present time, conciliation counseling is available in many large urban areas and only a handful of smaller communities. Moreover, even when it is available, information has been extremely scanty, and thus has not provided a basis upon which a prospective client (or her/his lawyer) can use mediation counseling as a meaningful alternative to the judicial process.

The second issue concerns the extent to which judicial processes for terminating marriage should reflect societal attitudes towards divorce. The rise in the divorce rate has been accompanied by significant attitudinal changes towards marital termination, including: the gradual disappearance of the stigma traditionally associated with divorce; the realization that the legal obstacles to divorce should not be such that ordinary couples who wish to terminate their marriage should be prevented from doing so; and, the recognition that even in its most friendly guise, divorce may become a destructive situation for both the spouses as well as for the children. From this perspective, the fact that litigation continues to be based on the adversarial system–a process which engenders fear, guilt, resentment and anger; which may be prohibitively expensive in both money and time; and which, by its very nature, pits spouse against spouse, parent against child–appears incongruent. In contrast, we suggest that when a marriage is over, it is not the time for retribution and revenge, but rather the occasion to strike out for a new life while providing for and protecting the children. For many couples, a non-adversarial process such as divorce mediation provides an effective means of achieving these ends.

"Of course, no judge can prevent parents from inflicting pain upon each other if they are determined to do so. No family relations officer can protect a child from being misused by warring parents. No attorney can enlighten a client who is unalterably committed to uncivilized values."[6] It is crucial that mediation procedures be made known to the public at large–to the married, the separated, the divorced and the divorcing. We cannot wait for the therapists and legal minds among us to change the system–it is for us to make those changes, it is our responsibility because too many, primarily our children, are losing out.

APPENDIX

How You Might Proceed

In point form, divorce mediation requires eight basic steps:

1. If there is any doubt about continuing the marriage, consult a qualified family or marriage counselor. Make sure she or he has proper credentials. Don't be embarrassed about this because any reputable counselor will be glad to produce them.

2. When the decision to divorce is made and a court-based service is what you want, call the local Family Court and ask for a conciliation or mediation appointment.

3. If private service is preferred, look in the telephone book for Mediation or Conciliation Services or ask the court to recommend some names to you. Recently, the courts have been compiling such lists. Again, ask for credentials.

4. When looking for a lawyer, find out whether he or she specializes in family law and has had any experience with mediators or arbitrators. If lawyers are permitted to advertise in your area, this information should be easy to get but if not, ask the courts or call the local Bar Association. Remember, just because a lawyer is recommended by family or friends doesn't mean he or she is experienced in family law. It is also advisable to ask the lawyer about his fees to prevent any later problems.

5. Work towards a mediated agreement, or ask for arbitration, and have the determination and courage to settle your own problems with qualified help.

6. Carry through and have your agreement or report validated by the court.

7. Go back to the mediator if further problems develop, or if changes are necessary.

Community Guidelines

If conciliation and mediation services are unavailable in your area, here are some guidelines to help in setting up such a program. They are general guidelines and need to be adapted to any particular location.

Conciliation Court Services

1. It is helpful for such a service to be imbued with the legal status and authority of the court system.

2. The service should be located within the court, so that they may be closely connected and to give the service greater credibility. This is especially important for lawyers making referrals.

3. Ideally the service should be provided on a state or province-wide basis and be jointly funded by state or province and federal levels of government.

4. A conciliation counselor should be available at all times to see an immediate referral following pre-trial conferences or referrals from judges.

5. There should be an advisory board made up of representatives from the professional and client communities.

6. A director of conciliation services should be appointed who is responsible to the chief judge or his designee.

7. Conciliation counseling should be made available to all who wish to make use of it, even before formal proceedings are instituted.

8. The service should perform both intake (initial screening) and dispute resolution functions in order to eliminate fragmentation and duplication of service.

9. There should be a conciliation team composed of social workers aided by consultation from lawyers, psychiatrists, and psychologists, as well as staff from the area's predominant social and ethnic groups.

10. The nature of the service should be short-term (approximately one to six interviews) and crisis-oriented, with dispute resolution as the mode of approach.

11. The service should be voluntary, but the court, through the use of its influence, should urge strongly that the service be used.

12. Conciliation counselors should have professional backgrounds in the psychological and social sciences with experience in family counseling and negotiating skills.

13. An intensive in-service training program should be established to provide seminars in the socio-legal implications of family law.

14. Students from various disciplines should be affiliated with the service for part of their clinical training.

15. In order to allow clients to discuss their problems openly, conciliation counselors should be granted privileged communication.

16. There should be opportunities for both mediation and arbitration depending upon the conciliator's assessment.

17. A research design should be developed prior to the establishment of a conciliation service, so that the service may be evaluated as it continues and so that further recommendations may be made.

Private Services (not Court Based)

1. A register of professionally qualified mediators should be established, the criteria set out by such bodies as the American Arbitration Association or a similar state or provincial body.

2. This service would be privately funded with a fee-for-service financial arrangement.

3. An on-going series of meetings between and among mediators, lawyers, and judges should be established.

4. The continuing process of divorce mediation should be in line with the court-based guidelines set out earlier.

The services of a mediator may be obtained by contacting the appropriate address on the following list. Although the list is up-to-date at press time, it doesn't include every community. Your local Association of Family Conciliation Courts will be able to supply you with specific information.

United States

Alaska

Family Resource Center
2311 Boniface Parkway
Anchorage, 99504

Superior Court — Trial Courts
Domestic Relations
Children's Matters
303 K Street
Anchorage 99501
(907) 274-8611, Ext. 521, 522

Arizona

PHOENIX (1964)
Conciliation Court
Maricopa County
Superior Court Building
101 West Jefferson Street
Second Floor
Phoenix 85003
(602) 262-3296

TUCSON (1963)
Conciliation Court
Pima County
Superior Court Building
2nd Floor
Tucson 85701
(602) 792-8468

California

ALAMEDA (1964)
Conciliation Court
1221 Oak Street
Oakland 94612
(415) 874-6284

CONTRA COSTA (1968)
The Conciliation Court
928 Main Street
Martinez, 94553
(415) 372-2681

FRESNO (1965)
Fresno County Family Court
229 Rowell Building
2100 Tulare Street
Fresno, 93721
(209) 488-3241

IMPERIAL (1959)
The Conciliation Court
Imperial County Courthouse
El Centro 92243
(714) 352-3610, Ext. 217

LOS ANGELES (1939)
The Conciliation Court
Room 241
111 North Hill Street
Los Angeles 90012
(213) 974-5524

NAPA (1974)
Conciliation Court
Superior Court of Napa County
730A Randolph Street
Napa 94558
(707) 253-4206

RIVERSIDE (1977)
The Conciliation Court
Superior Court,
Riverside County
4050 Main Street, Suite 104
Riverside 92501
(784) 787-2788
(714) 342-8379 (Indio)

SACRAMENTO (1962)
Office of Family Court Services
Room 603, Courthouse
720 9th Street
Sacramento, 95814
(916) 440-4533

SAN BERNARDINO (1961)
The Conciliation Court
Courthouse Annex, First Floor
San Bernardino 92415
(714) 383-1966

SAN DIEGO (1963)
The Conciliation Court
110 W. C St., Suite 1301
Charter Oil Bldg.
San Diego 92101
(714) 236-2681

SAN FRANCISCO (1950)
Domestic Relations Court
Room 463, City Hall
San Francisco 94102
(415) 558-4186

SAN MATEO (1960)
Court of Conciliation
Hall of Justice and Records
Redwood City 94063
(415) 364-5600

SANTA CLARA (1967)
The Conciliation Court
County of Santa Clara
Superior Court Building
San Jose 95113
(408) 299-3741

SAN JOAQUIN (1967)
Conciliation Court
Courthouse—Room 370
Stockton 95202
(209) 944-2355

SHASTA (1969)
The Conciliation Court
Cascade Office Building
2430 Hospital Lane
Room 47
Redding 96001
(916) 246-5707

SONOMA (1969)
The Conciliation Court
Hall of Justice
Santa Rosa 95401
(707) 527-2765

Hawaii
HONOLULU (1966)
Family Court
1st Circuit
P.O. Box 3498
Judiciary Building
Honolulu 96811
(808) 548-7661

Illinois
CHICAGO (1965)
Conciliation Service
Circuit Court of Cook County
Daley Center, Suite 1901
Chicago 60602
(312) 443-7914

Michigan
DETROIT (1948)
Family Counseling Service of
  Wayne County Circuit Court
Third Judicial Circuit of
  Michigan
900 W. Lafayette Avenue
Detroit 48226
(313) 224-5266

Minnesota
MINNEAPOLIS
Hennepin County Family Court
5-C Government Center
Minneapolis 55487
(612) 348-5070

Domestic Relations Division
A503 Government Center
Minneapolis 55487
(612) 348-7556

Domestic Relations Division
1745 Court House
St. Paul 55102
(612) 298-4379

ST. PAUL
Ramsey County Family Court
1700 Court House
St. Paul 55102
(612) 298-4875

Montana
BOZEMAN (1963)
Conciliation Court
Eighteenth Judicial District
P.O. Box 1050
Bozeman 59715
(406) 587-4331

GREAT FALLS (1967)
Court of Conciliation
Eighth Judicial District
325 Second Avenue North
111 Thisted Center
P.O. Box 1466
Great Falls 59403
(406) 761-6700, Ext. 254

KALISPELL (1973)
Family Court Services
Eleventh Judicial District
P.O. Box 105
Kalispell 59901
(406) 755-5300, Ext. 348

Nebraska
LINCOLN (1966)
The Conciliation Court
County-City Building
Lincoln 68508
(402) 473-6429

OMAHA (1967)
The Conciliation Court
416 Keeline Building
17th and Harney
Omaha 68102
(402) 444-7168 or 444-7169

New York
American Arbitration
  Association
140 West 15th Street
New York, N.Y. 10020

North Carolina
Family Mediation Association
Suite 735 First Union Building
310 West Fourth Street
Winston-Salem, N.C.

Oregon
CLACKAMAS COUNTY (1976)
Family Court Service
Suite 305
704 Main Street
Oregon City 97045
(503) 655-8415

COQUILLE (1967)
Conciliation Services
Circuit Court
Coquille 97423
(503) 396-3121

PORTLAND (1964)
Family Services
Court of Domestic Relations
Room 350
Multnomah County Courthouse
Portland 97204
(503) 248-3189

SALEM (1966)
Conciliation Services
Department of Domestic
  Relations

Circuit Court
Salem 97301
(503) 588-5088

Washington
EVERETT
Family Court Division
Court of Domestic Relations
2801 — 10th Street
Everett 98201
(206) 259-0031

KELSO (1949)
Family Court
Hall of Justice
312 South 1st Avenue West
Kelso 98626
(206) 577-3076

PORT ORCHARD (1969)
Family Court
Kitsap County Courthouse
Port Orchard 98366
(206) 876-4441
(206) 478-4585 (KCCS)

SEATTLE (1950)
Family Court
W-364 King County Courthouse
Seattle 98104
(206) 344-2670

TACOMA (1949)
Family Court
950 Fawcett Avenue, Suite 211
Tacoma 98402
(206) 593-4495

Wisconsin
MADISON
Dane County Family Court
  Counseling Service
Room 311-A City-County
  Building
Madison 53709
(608) 266-4607

MILWAUKEE (1933)
Family Court
Circuit Court
Department of Family
  Conciliation
Room 711, Courthouse
Milwaukee 53233
(414) 278-4428

Canada

Alberta

Edmonton Conciliation Court
500 Century Plaza
9803-102A Avenue
Edmonton T5J 3A6

British Columbia

Langley Probation & Fam.
  Services
20618 Eastleigh Crescent
Langley V3A 4C4

Court Services Division
  Ministry of Atty-General
5th Fl., 850 Burdett Avenue
Victoria V8W 1B4

Unified Family Court
4465 Clarence Taylor Crescent
Delta V4K 3W4

Ministry of the Atty-General
West Family & Juv. Prob.
#101-3540 West 41st Avenue
Vancouver V6N 3E6

Victoria Family Court
British Columbia Correction
  Services
2020 Cameron Street
Victoria

Manitoba

Juvenile & Family Court
Building 30-139 Tuxedo Avenue
Winnipeg R3N 0H6

New Brunswick

Family Court Services
P.O. Box 6398 - "A"
Saint John E2L 4R8

Ontario

Unified Family Court
100 James St. S.
Hamilton L8P 2Z3

Frontenac Family Referral
  Service
P.O. Box 981
469 Montreal Street
Kingston K7L 4X8

Conciliation Project
311 Jarvis Street
Toronto M5B 2C4

Saskatchewan

Family Service Bureau of Regina
1801 Toronto St.
Regina S4P 1M7

Unified Family Court
311 - 21st St. East
Saskatoon S7K 0C1

NOTES AND REFERENCES

Chapter 1

1. Extracted in part from an earlier paper by H. Irving and B. Irving, "Conciliation Counselling in Divorce Litigation," *Reports of Family Law* 16 (1974): 257-266.

2. Irving N. Griswold, quoted by Meyer Elkin in "How the Social Worker can Assist the Attorney in Rehabilitating Broken Marriages," in N. Kohut, Ed., *Therapeutic Family Law* (Chicago: Family Law Publications, 1968), p. 194.

3. Quoted from a booklet entitled "Stress and the Divorced," published by Hoffmann-LaRoche Limited, Vaudreuil, Quebec.

4. Louis H. Burke, quoted by Paul McLane Conway, in "To Insure Domestic Tranquility: Reconciliation Services as an Alternative to the Divorce Attorney," *Journal of Family Law* 60 (1970): 411.

5. Meyer Elkin presents a thoughtful view of this difficult situation in "Editorial," *Conciliation Courts Review* 15 (December 1977): iii-iv.

6. Ibid.

7. The authors present a comprehensive theory of the family as a social system: William Lederer and Don Jackson, *The Mirages of Marriage* (New York: W. W. Norton and Co., 1968), p. 14.

Chapter 2

1. O. J. Coogler's article "Changing the Lawyer's Role in Matrimonial Practice" sets out the lawyer's role in a clear and direct way pointing out some major role conflicts: Lois Forer, quoted by O. J. Coogler, in "Changing the Lawyer's Role in Matrimonial Practice," *Conciliation Courts Review* 15 (September 1977): 3.

2. Robert Weiss, quoted by O. J. Coogler, in "Changing the Lawyer's Role in Matrimonial Practice," *Conciliation Courts Review* 15 (September 1977): 3.

3. Herbert Glieberman, quoted by O. J. Coogler, in "Changing the Lawyer's Role in Matrimonial Practice," *Conciliation Courts Review* 15 (September 1977): 2-3.

4. Margaret Rosenheim: "The Lawyer As A Family Counselor–As The Social Worker Sees Him," *University of Kansas City Law Review* 22 (1953): 28.

5. Paul Conway, "To Insure Domestic Tranquility–Reconciliation Services As An Alternative To The Divorce Attorney," *Journal of Family Law* 9 (1970): 408.

6. Susan Gettleman and Janet Markowitz, quoted by O. J. Coogler, in "Changing the Lawyer's Role in Matrimonial Practice," *Conciliation Courts Review* 15 (September 1977): 4.

Chapter 3

1. This helpful material on the Jewish Conciliation Court was extracted in part from: James Yaffe, *So Sue Me* (New York: Saturday Review Press, 1972), pp. 12-13, 267-268.

2. Frank Gibney, "10,000 Lawyers vs. 350,000," *Center Report of the Center for the Study of Democratic Institutions* (1975), pp. 1-10.

3. This account follows an observation of the Chinese People's Court by Elliot and his Canadian legal colleagues: R. M. Elliot, "Divorce Chinese Style," *The Advocate* 37 (June-July 1979): pp. 318-319.

4. Ibid.

5. H. Irving, et al., "A Comparative Analysis of Two Family Court Services: An Exploratory Study of Conciliation Counseling," Ministry of the Attorney General of Ontario, 1979, p. 5.

6. Meyer Elkin, "Conciliation Courts: The Reintegration of Disintegrating Families," *The Family Coordinator* 22 (January 1973).

7. O. J. Coogler, *Structured Mediation in Divorce Settlement* (Lexington, Mass.: D. C. Heath & Co., 1978).

8. K. Eckhardt, "Deviancy, Visibility, and Legal Action: The Duty To Support" in *Deviancy and the Family.* C. Bryant and J. Wells, Eds., Philadelphia, 1973.

9. Law Reform Commission of Canada: Family Law: Enforcement of Maintenance Obligations, 1976.

Chapter 4

1. Howard Irving, *The Family Myth* (Toronto: Copp Clark Publishing Co., 1972).

2. M. Roman and W. Haddad, *The Disposable Parent* (New York: Holt, Rinehart and Winston, 1978), p. 54.

3. Joseph Epstein, *Divorced in America* (New York: Penguin Books Inc., 1974), p. 263.

4. T. H. Holmes and R. H. Rahe, "Social Readjustment Rating Scale," *Journal of Psychosomatic Research* 2 (1967): 213.

5. Reva Wiseman, "Crisis Theory and the Process of Divorce," *Social Casework* 56 (April 1975): 205-212.

6. Adelaide Ferguson, "The Divorce Experience," *Conciliation Courts Review* 16 (June 1978): 33-34.

7. J. Westman and S. Cline, "Divorce is a Family Affair," *Reports of Family Law* 4 (1972): 310-318.

8. M. Roman and W. Haddad, *The Disposable Parent* (New York: Holt, Rinehart and Winston, 1978), p. 75.

9. Cynthia Longfellow, "Divorce in Context: Its Impact on Children," in *Divorce and Separation*, George Levinger and Oliver Moles, Eds., (New York: Basic Books Inc., 1979), pp. 305-306.

10. B. Berg and R. Kelly, "The Measured Self-Esteem of Children from Broken, Rejected, and Accepted Families," *Journal of Divorce* 2 (Summer 1979): p. 364.

11. Ibid., p. 366.

12. Draft Report on "Conciliation," Ministry of Attorney General Ontario, December, 1979, pp. 36-37.

13. The Bill of Rights of Children in Divorce Actions quoted by Barbara Chisholm in "Should Judges Interview Children?," Canadian Council on Children and Youth, Vol. 2, pp. 11-12.

Chapter 6

1. Some of this material is extracted from an earlier publication: E. Lightman and H. Irving, "Conciliation and Arbitration in Family Disputes," *Conciliation Courts Review* 14 (1976): 12-21.

2. This type of referral letter utilized by one of the lawyers was originally developed by James C. MacDonald, Q.C.

3. J. Goldstein, A. Freud, and R. Solnit, *Beyond the Best Interests of the Child* (New York: Free Press, 1973).

4. J. B. Kelley and J. S. Wallerstein, "Part-Time Parent, Part-Time Child: Visiting After Divorce," *Journal of Clinical Child Psychology* 6 (1977): 54.

5. E. M. Hetherington, M. Cox, and R. Cox, "Divorced Fathers," *Family Coordinator* (1976): 25, 417-428.

6. Rhona Rosen, "Children of Divorce: What They Feel About Access and Other Aspects of the Divorce Experience," *Journal of Clinical Child Psychology* (Summer 1977): 26.

7. G. Berman and L. Berman, "Comments on the Law of Access," *Reports of Family Law* 9 (September 1979): 74.

8. Janet Spencer and Joseph Zammit, "Reflections on Arbitration under the Family Dispute Services," *The Arbitration Journal* 32 (June 1977): 111.

Chapter 8

1. H. Irving and B. Schlesinger, "Canada's Other Lottery," in *The Child and the Courts*, edited by I. Baxter and M. Eberts Carswell, 1978.

2. D. Orthner and K. Lewis, "Evidence of Single Father Competence in Child Rearing," in *Family Law Quarterly* 13 (Spring 1979): 29.

3. Joseph Epstein, *Divorced in America* (New York: Penguin Books, 1974), p. 191.

4. D. Orthner and K. Lewis, "Evidence of Single Father Competence in Child Rearing," in *Family Law Quarterly* 13 (Spring 1979): 45.

5. Rhona Rosen, "Children of Divorce: What They Feel about Access and other Aspects of the Divorce Experience," *Journal of Clinical Child Psychology* (Summer 1977): 24-27.

6. The case material and judicial decisions are extracted from D. Siegel and S. Hunley, "The Role of the Child's Preference in Custody Procedures," *Family Law Quarterly* 11 (Spring 1977): 12-13.

7. Ibid., p. 14.

8. Ibid., p. 15.

9. This author has written three important monographs on children and the law: Barbara A. Chisholm, "Should Judges Interview Children?," The Child as Citizen–Canadian Council on Children, p. 5.

10. Wayne Clark, "Divorce By Fire," in *Weekend Magazine*, June 5, 1967.

11. Henry Foster and Doris Freed quoted by Barbara Chisholm, "Should Judges Interview Children?," The Child as Citizen–Canadian Council on Children, p. 7-8.

12. Much of this material is extracted from the article by Kim Landsman and Martha Minow which is one of the few research studies on the subject. "Lawyering for the Child: Principles of Representation in Custody and Visitation Disputes Arising from Divorce," *The Yale Law Journal* 87 (1978): 1126.

13. Ibid., p. 1126-1190.

14. Extracted from an unreported child welfare case; Judge R. S. Abella, Provincial Court (Family Division) of the Judicial District of York.

15. Justice Lieff, "Pre-Trial of Family Law in The Supreme Court: Simplify and Expedite," *The Law Society Gazette* (December 1976).

16. Much of this material is extracted from the article by Kim Landsman and Martha Minow which is one of the few research studies on the subject. "Lawyering for the Child: Principles of Representation in Custody and Visitation Disputes Arising from Divorce," *The Yale Law Journal* 87 (1978): 1186-1187.

Chapter 9

1. Most of the material in this chapter is extracted from an unpublished paper "Critical Aspects of the Lawyer-Client Interview," presented at a continuing education conference for The Upper Canada Law Society in July, 1977 by Barbara Irving and Howard Irving.

2. Gary S. Goodpaster, "Human Arts of Lawyering: Interviewing and Counseling," *The Journal of Legal Education* 27 (1975): 50.

Chapter 10

1. Frederick G. Gans, "The Non-custodial Parent. A Personal View," a monograph published by the Department of Continuing Education, The Law Society of Upper Canada, Osgoode Hall, Toronto.

2. Elizabeth G. Baldwin, quotes Judge Shea in "Joint Custody: A Consideration of New Patterns of Allocating Custody and Care and Control of Children," Unpublished Paper, 1979, pp. 26-27.

3. "The Worth of Joint Custody," as reprinted in the *Globe and Mail*, May 24, 1979.

Chapter 11

1. Morton Deutsch is one of the leaders in developing the theory of conflict resolution. Morton Deutsch, *The Resolution of Conflict* (New Haven: Yale University Press, 1973), p. 351.

2. Ibid., p. 352.

3. Ibid., p. 353.

4. H. Irving et al., "A Study of Conciliatory Counseling in the Family Court of Toronto," Unpublished Paper, (March 1980): 32.

5. Taken from a letter sent to board members of the Association of Family Conciliation Courts by Judge Betty Barteau.

6. Joseph L. Steinberg, quoted in the *Hartford Courant*, January 4, 1980.

BIBLIOGRAPHY

Alberta Conciliation Service, *Demonstration Project #558-1-12, National Health and Welfare Canada,* 1975.

American Bar Association. "Proposed Revised Uniform Marriage and Divorce Act." *Family Law Quarterly* 7 (1973): 135-165.

Atkin, Edith, and Rubin, Estelle. *Part Time Father.* New York: Vanguard Press, 1976.

Baum, C. "Divided Custody." *New York Times Magazine* (Oct. 31, 1976).

Benedek, E. B., and Benedek, R. S. "New Child Custody Laws: Making Them Do What They Say." *American Journal of Orthopedic Medicine* 42 (1972): 825-834.

Black, Melvin, and Joffee, Wendy. "A Lawyer/Therapist Approach to Divorce." *Conciliation Courts Review* 16 (1978): 1-8.

Bohannan, Paul, ed. *Divorce and After.* Garden City, N.Y.: Doubleday, 1970.

Brim, Orville G., et al. *Personality and Decision Processes: Studies in the Social Psychology of Thinking.* Stanford, California: Stanford University Press, 1962.

Brown, P., and Manela, R. "Client Satisfaction with Marital and Divorce Counselling." *The Family Coordinator* (July 1977): 294-303.

Callner, Bruce W. "Boundaries of the Divorce Lawyer's Role." *Family Law Quarterly* 10 (1977): 389-398.

Chiancola, S. P. "The Process of Separation and Divorce: A New Approach." *Social Casework* 59 (1978): 494-499.

Chiriboga, D. A., and Cutler, L. "Stress Responses Among Divorcing Men and Women." *Journal of Divorce* 1 (1977): 95-106.

Coogler, O. J. "Changing the Lawyer's Role in Matrimonial Practice." *Conciliation Courts Review* 15 (1977): 1-8.

Despert, J. Louise. *Children of Divorce*. Garden City, N.Y.: Doubleday, 1962.

Deutsch, Morton. *The Resolution of Conflict*. New Haven, Conn.: Yale University Press, 1973.

Elkin, M., "Conciliation Courts: The Reintegration of Disintegrating Families." *The Family Coordinator* 22 (January 1973): 63-72.

Epstein, Joseph. *Divorced in America: Marriage in an Age of Possibility*. New York: Penguin Books, 1975.

Framo, James L. "The Friendly Divorce." *Psychology Today* (February 1978): 77-102.

Freed, D. J., and Foster, H. H., Jr. "The Shuffled Child and the Divorce Court." *Trial* 10 (1974): 26-41.

_____. "Taking Out the Fault But Not the Sting." *Trial* 12 (1976): 10-19.

Frontenac Family Referral Service. *Couples in Crisis*. Kingston, Ontario: Frontenac Family Referral Service, 1979.

Fuller, Lon L. "Mediation." *Southern California Law Review* 9 (Fall 1974): 305-339.

Galper, Miriam. *Co-Parenting: Sharing Your Child Equally*. Philadelphia: The Running Press, 1978.

Gardner, G. "Separation of the Parents and the Emotional Life of the Child." *Mental Hygiene* 40 (1956): 27-45.

Gardner, R. A. *Psychotherapy with Children of Divorce*. New York: Jason Aronson, Inc., 1976.

Gibney, Frank Bray. "10,000 Lawyers Vs. 350,000." *Center Report* of the Center for the Study of Democratic Institutions (1975): 1-10.

Glasser, Claire L. "A Case for Counselling in Child Custody Cases." *Conciliation Courts Review* 13 (1975): 12-13.

Goldstein, Joseph; Freud, Anna; and Solnit, Albert J. *Beyond the Best Interests of the Child*. New York: Free Press Division of McMillan, 1973.

Haynes, J. M. "Divorce Mediator: A new Role." *Social Work* 23 (1978): 5-9.

Hetherington, E. M.; Cox, M.; and Cox, R. "Divorced Fathers." *Family Coordinator* 25 (1976): 417-428.

Holmes, T. H. and Rahe, R. H. "The Social Readjustment Rating Scale." *Journal of Psychosomatic Research* 11 (1967): 213-218.

Hunt, M., and Hunt, B. *The Divorce Experience.* New York: McGraw-Hill, 1977.

Hunt, M. *The World of the Formerly Married.* New York: McGraw-Hill, 1966.

Irving, Howard H. *The Family Myth.* Toronto: Copp Clark, 1972.

Irving, Howard H., and Bohm, P. "A Social Science Approach to Family Dispute Resolution." *Canadian Journal of Family Law* 1 (1978): 39-56.

Irving, Howard H., and Gandy, John. "Family Court Conciliation Project: An Experiment in Support Services." *Reports of Family Law* 25 (1977): 47-53.

Irving, Howard H., and Irving, Barbara G. "Conciliation Counselling in Divorce Litigation." *Reports of Family Law* 16 (1974): 257-266.

Irving, Howard H., et al. *A Comparative Analysis of Two Family Court Services: An Exploratory Study of Conciliatory Counselling.* Toronto: Ministry of the Attorney General, Ontario, 1979.

Kelly, J. B., and Wallerstein, J. S. "The Effects of Parental Divorce: Experiences of the Child in Early Latency." *American Journal of Orthopsychiatry* 46 (1976): 20.

———. "Part-Time Parent, Part-Time Child: Visiting After Divorce." *Journal of Clinical Psychology* 6 (1977): 51-54.

Kenniston, K. All Our Children: *The American Family Under Pressure.* New York: Harcourt Brace Jovanovich, 1977.

Kressel, Kenneth K., et al. "Mediated Negotiation in Divorce and Labor Disputes: A Comparison." *Conciliation Courts Review* 15 (1977): 1-12.

Kressel, K., and Deutsch, M. "Divorce Therapy: An In-Depth Survey of Therapists' Views." *Family Process* 16 (1977): 413-443.

Lawrence, W. "Divided Custody of Children After Their Parents Divorce." *Journal of Family Law* (1968).

Lederer, William J., and Jackson, Dr. Don D. *The Mirages of Marriage.* New York: W. W. Norton & Company, 1968.

Lightman, E. S., and Irving, H. H. "Conciliation and Arbitration in Family Disputes." *Conciliation Courts Review* 14 (1976): 12-21.

Rheinstein, Max. *Marriage Stability, Divorce, and the Law.* Chicago: University of Chicago Press, 1972.

Roman, M. and Haddad, W. *The Disposable Parent.* New York: Holt, Rinehart and Winston, 1978.

Rosen, R. "Children of Divorce: What They Feel About Access and Other Aspects of the Divorce Experience." *Journal of Clinical Child Psychology* 6 (1977): 24-27.

Rosenheim, Margaret K. "The Lawyer as a Family Counselor: As the Social Worker Sees Him." *University of Kansas City Law Review* 22 (1953): 28.

Rubin, Jeffrey A., and Brown, Bert R. *The Social Psychology of Bargaining and Negotiation.* New York: Academic Press, 1975.

Schlesinger, B. "The One-Parent Family in Perspective." In B. Schlesinger (ed.). *The One-Parent Family.* Toronto: University of Toronto Press, 1969.

Wallerstein, Judith, and Kelly, Joan. "The Effects of Parental Divorce: The Adolescent Experience." *The Child and His Family* 3 (1974).

Wallerstein, Judith, and Kelly, Joan. "The Effects of Parental Divorce: Experiences of the Pre-School Child." *Journal of the American Academy of Child Psychiatry* 14 (Autumn 1975): 600-616.

Weiss, Robert S. *Marital Separation.* New York: Basic Books, 1975.

Weiss, W. W., and Collada, H. B. "Conciliation Counselling: The Court's Effective Mechanism for Resolving Visitation and Custody Disputes." *The Family Coordinator* 26 (1977): 444-447.

Wheeler, M. *No-Fault Divorce.* Boston: Beacon Press, 1974.

Women in Transition, Inc. *Women in Transition: A Feminist Handbook on Separation and Divorce.* New York: Scribner's, 1975.

Yaffe, James. *So Sue Me.* New York: Saturday Review Press, 1972.

INDEX

213

Index